D0056759

CLASSIC PUZZLES

THIS IS A CARLTON BOOK

Published in 2018 by Carlton Books Limited
an imprint of the Carlton Publishing Group
20 Mortimer Street
London W1T 3JW

A catalogue record for this book is available from the British Library

ISBN 978-1-78739-097-3

Printed in Dubai

10 9 8 7 6 5 4 3 2 1

Content previously published in *The Greatest Puzzles Ever Solved*

CLASSIC PUZZLES

From
ANCIENT EGYPT
to the
MODERN ERA

TIM DEDOPULOS

CARLTON BOOKS

CONTENTS

INTRODUCTION

Puzzles are one of the areas of human experience that transcend all cultural barriers. Every nation on Earth has puzzles, and probably has done for as long as humankind has been able to reason. Faced with the unknown, our natural curiosity drives us to find some sort of resolution. When we know that the mystery has been set in front of us as a test, the urge to solve it – to prove ourselves – becomes almost unbearable.

Deduction is probably mankind's single greatest tool. The ability to reason and theorize – to connect cause and effect into a model of the world – has led us from the early caves to our current society of wonders. Without it, there would be no technological progress, no real understanding of others, no written language... no humanity. Our capacity for logical reasoning is the main quality that separates us from the rest of the animals. So perhaps it's no surprise that we all get enjoyment from exercising that ability.

Puzzles give us the chance to exercise our mental muscles. That is not just a metaphor; in many important senses, it is a literal description of the way our minds work. Push your mind's limits, and your brainpower will get stronger, more flexible, faster – fitter. Ignore it, and it will get weaker and flabbier, exactly the same way that a body does. Recent scientific discoveries have shown that the brain really does respond to mental exercise, and solving puzzles can even help to stave off the effects of diseases like Alzheimer's.

The parallels between physical and mental exercise run deeper, too. Like physical exercise, mental exercise gives us a sense of achievement, improves our mood, and can give us a lot of pleasure. Achievement in puzzle solving and logical thought can even be a mark of status, similar to that of an athlete. In China and Japan, mental agility has been regarded as a highly skilled competitive sport for centuries, with some of the top stars becoming household names.

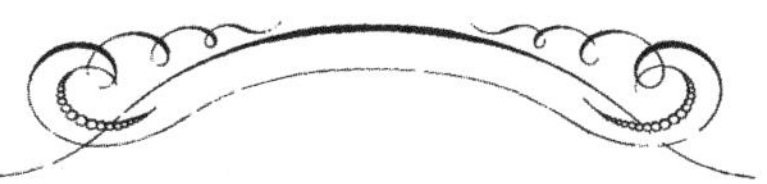

A Historical Overview of Puzzling

Ever since humans have been thinkers, there have been puzzles to stimulate and exercise the mind. The earliest puzzle identified originated in ancient Babylonia, and dates to around 2000BC. It involves working out the lengths of the sides of a triangle. From then on, the preserved record of our puzzle activity gets steadily stronger. The Rhind Papyrus is an ancient Egyptian riddle that is thought to come from much the same sort of time. A few hundred years later, Phoenician puzzle jugs – which required some lateral thinking to fill and drink from – became popular. By 1200BC, dice had been invented. This innovation occurred during the long, dull siege of Troy if the legends are to be believed.

A well-documented craze for lateral thinking and logical deduction puzzles and riddles swept through ancient Greece from the 5th century BC, lasting for several hundred years. That carried on over into ancient Rome in the form of advanced mathematical and logical work. The Chinese invented Magic Square puzzles around 100BC, calling them "Lo Shu", river maps. Other Chinese puzzle advances followed, including the first sets of interlocking puzzle rings around 300AD, the game of Snakes and Ladders by 700AD, and the first versions of playing cards in 969AD, with a deck of cards made for the Emperor Mu-Tsung. However, the deck of cards we know now almost certainly came from Persia some hundred years later, arriving into Europe with Spanish sailors.

The puzzle game of Fox and Hounds arose in the 12th century in Scandinavia. Despite rumours of antiquity, Tangrams – one of the most famous Chinese puzzles – remained unknown before 1727AD, making them a comparatively recent innovation. After the close of the American Revolution in the late 18th century, new print and literature flooded the new nation, word problems seeing particular popularity, especially those that played with formation and pronunciation of said language.

Since these eras past, new, innovative puzzles have risen to be the most popular forms. Whether they are the crossword or Sudoku puzzle, they have been built on the foundations that these classic puzzles have formed over centuries of erudite creation. Revisiting the puzzles that grand, ancient civilizations mulled over is as useful as looking over any modern word problem or riddle, and can give an insight into the thinking behind the worlds that we only see echoes of in ruins and archeological digs today.

Tim Dedopulos

8

THE ISHANGO BONE

The Ishango tribe lived in Zaire in Africa around 9000BC, and may have been amongst the forefathers of modern African people. Out of all the many archaeological discoveries that have been made regarding the Ishango, perhaps the most significant is a small tool, made out of a bone handle with a chunk of quartz set into the end. It's thought that the Ishango Bone was used for inscription of some sort – perhaps engraving, maybe even writing. That alone would make it fascinating. But the Ishango Bone contains three sets of numbers, in the forms of columns of scratches marked into its sides. Although there remains some academic uncertainty, it is thought that each of the three groups represents a depiction of the tribe's knowledge of mathematical processes – astonishing, given the era. The first column is the plainest. There is a 3 next to a 6, a 4 next to an 8, and a 10 next to a 5, along with a further 5 and a 7. Leaving aside the last pair for the moment, these pairs clearly indicate multiplication by two.

What mathematical processes do the other two sides indicate, and where do the remaining 5 and 7 from the first side fit?

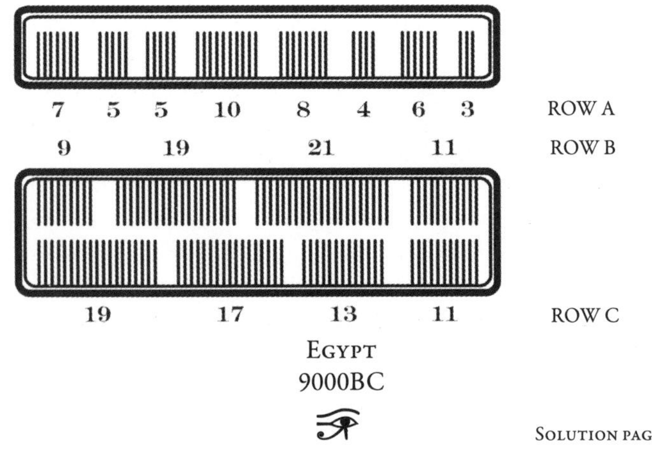

EGYPT
9000BC

SOLUTION PAGE 102

HOLY DAYS

The ancient Egyptian cult of Isis began some time before 2500BC, and survived into ancient Greece and Rome. Isis was the goddess of fertility and motherhood, and her husband, Osiris, was the god of the underworld. Lunar symbolism was central to the cult, which believed that Osiris had been murdered and dismembered, before being (mostly) put back together by Isis, who then resurrected him.

Members of the cult of Isis believed that Osiris had been killed on the 17th of the lunar month, the point at which the moon's waning becomes obvious. As a result, that day – and number – was abominable, ritually taboo. By contrast, 28, the length of the lunar month, was sacred, and Osiris was said to have reigned (or sometimes lived) for 28 years. Osiris was even said to have been chopped into 14 parts, representing the 14 days of the moon's waning.

The cult also held two other numbers in esteem however – the only two possible whole-number perimeter values of a rectangle which encloses the same area as its own length. Which two numbers are they, and why else might they have been important to the cult?

EGYPT
2000BC

SOLUTION PAGE 102

Frustrum

The Moscow Papyrus is the oldest known Egyptian mathematical text. It is thought to date to some time shortly before 2000BC, making it somewhat older than its longer, more detailed cousin, the *Rhind Papyrus*. *The Moscow Papyrus* was purchased, contents unknown, by Egyptologist Vladimir Goleniscev around the end of the 19th century, and then re-sold to the Pushkin Museum in 1909. The scribe responsible for the Moscow Papyrus did not record his name, but the manuscript is also sometimes known as the *Goleniscev Mathematical Papyrus*. Problem 14 of the *Moscow Papyrus* poses this unusually sophisticated question:

If you are told that a truncated square-base pyramid has 6 for the vertical height, by 4 on the base and by 2 on the top, what is the volume?

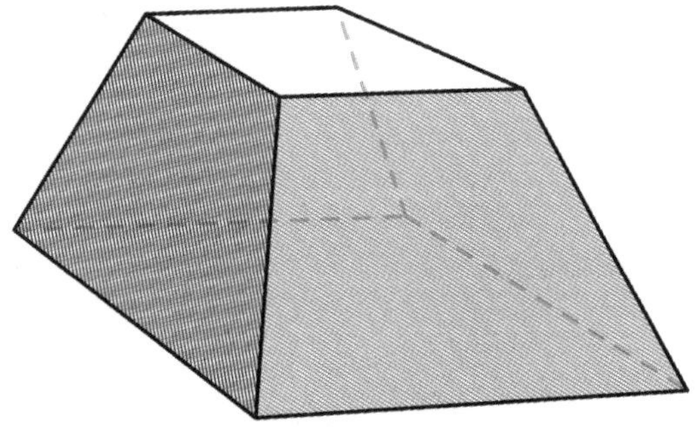

Egypt
1950BC

Solution page 103

11

TRIANGLES OF BABYLON

This puzzle is taken from a Babylonian clay tablet dating from around 1900BC, found in the Schoyen Collection – a wonderful treasury of philanthropically-assembled manuscripts of all types from the last five millennia – and gives an interesting geometric problem. It is thought that the tablet might have been something in the nature of an assignment for students, because it doesn't give the answer to the problem.

As you can see in the image, two equilateral triangles are nested in one another, parallel on all sides. The smaller has a side length of three; the larger, 5. What is the area of the space between the two triangles?

BABYLONIA
1900BC

SOLUTION PAGE 103

12

AHMES' LOAVES

The oldest remaining collection of puzzles known to us is a collection of mathematical problems from ancient Egypt. It was written in 1650BC by a scribe named Ahmes, working from now-lost parchments that were at least 200 years older, and may have even dated from times before that. The collection is known as the *Rhind Papyrus*, after the Scotsman who bought the document, as an Egyptian curio, in the 1850s. The *Rhind Papyrus* provides us with an invaluable insight into Egyptian mathematical techniques and logical thought. One of the more interesting peculiarities of the Egyptian system was their method of subdividing whole numbers. They understood the idea of fractions, to a sophisticated degree, but did not have any conception of fractional multiples. In other words, they understood the idea of ¼ easily, but the idea of ¾ was totally alien. In fact, even the idea of repeating the same fraction for one given number would have confused them. So if an ancient Egyptian subtracted ¼ from 1, he would not have thought of the remainder as ¾, or even as ¼ + ¼ + ¼, but as ½ + ¼.

Bearing that in mind, one of Ahmes' puzzles asks the reader to divide three loaves of bread between five men. What solution would he have understood? It will help if you think about the problem practically – each man must receive not only the same amount of bread, but also the same type and number of pieces, each of which must be a different size.

Egypt
1850BC

Solution page 104

13

As I Was Going to Amenemhet III's

The best-known puzzle in the *Rhind Papyrus* is famous primarily because it has survived down through the centuries, travelling via Rome to end up in 18th century Europe and on to the modern era. The Rhind version barely bothers to give the question, concentrating instead on the answer, presumably because the question was already so well-known. Everything considered, it has aged remarkably well.

A wealthy priest owns seven houses. Each of these houses contains seven cats. Each cat must eat seven mice, because each mouse can eat seven sheaves of wheat. A sheaf of wheat can produce seven hekats of grain. Houses, cats, mice, sheaves, grain: how many in total fall within the priest's domain?

Egypt
1850BC

Solution page 104

14

A Question of Quantity

In Problem 24 of the *Rhind Papyrus*, Ahmes asks the reader to calculate a missing quantity:

One amount added to a quarter of that amount becomes 15. What is the amount?

Egypt
1850BC

Solution page 105

A Fractional Issue

Ahmes presents a number of problems in the *Rhind Papyrus* that are clearly meant to give instruction and practice with the issue of doubling any given unit fraction. As $^2/_3$ was the only allowed fraction that wasn't 1/#, and repeating a fraction within a single number wasn't allowed, this was a somewhat thorny issue. Ahmes presented a table of fractions and their doubles – $^1/_5$, for example, doubled to $^1/_3 + ^1/_{15}$ – but we have modern techniques instead.

Problem 21 of the *Rhind Papyrus* asks the reader to complete $^2/_3 + ^1/_{15}$ to 1. Can you do it following the Egyptian rules?

Egypt
1850BC

Solution page 105

16

STRONG GRAIN

Ahmes sets this puzzle involving equivalent values in Problem 72 of the *Rhind Papyrus*. We can quickly recognize that the problem is one of percentages, but that was not a concept that fitted readily with the Egyptian mathematical system.

A group of men have 100 hekats of barley of impurity (pesu) 10. They wish to exchange it for a fair quantity of inferior barley, of pesu 45. What is the fair quantity?

EGYPT
1850BC

SOLUTION PAGE 106

17

PROGRESSIVE LOAVES

The mathematical rule of *Regula Falsi* (or False Position) states that, when attempting to solve a mathematical problem, if you put in a value that you know to give the wrong answer, the proportion of the wrong answer to the answer you want should indicate the proportion by which your initial value is incorrect. As a very trivial example, look at the question x*3 = 6. Try x=1, and you get 1*3 = 3. You need to double 3 to get 6, so you need to double 1 to get the right answer, 2. Obvious here, but more useful when the question is complex, although you might need to try two or three progressive possibilities to see a clear trend.

In the *Rhind Papyrus*, Ahmes lists a question that, at the time at least, required quite sophisticated use of the *Regula Falsi* in order to be solved.

100 loaves are to be divided unevenly between five men. The amount of bread received by each man decreases by the same amount each time, and the last two men's shares together are equal to just $^1/_7$ of the first three's collected shares. By how much do the shares decrease each time?

EGYPT
1850BC

SOLUTION PAGE 106

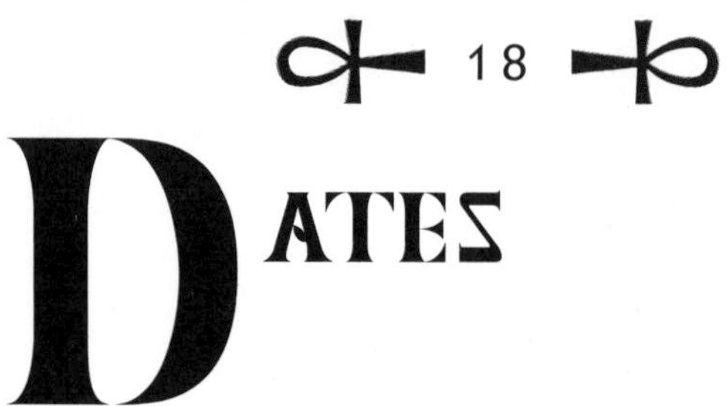

18 DATES

Some of the questions in the *Rhind Papyrus* can get quite complex, particularly given the mathematics of the time. For some, the key really does lie in finding the best available technique for cracking the nut of the problem, rather than settling for a less ideal method of solution.

Bear Egyptian mathematical peculiarities in mind as you consider Problem 28 of the Papyrus. A quantity together with its two-thirds has one third of its sum taken away to yield 10. What is the quantity?

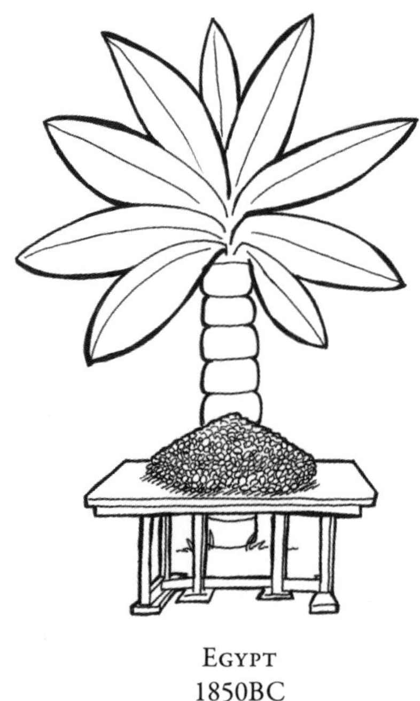

EGYPT
1850BC

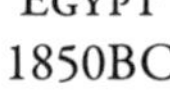

SOLUTION PAGE 107

THE RULE OF THREE

The 24th puzzle of the *Rhind Papyrus* provides an interesting example of a problem and solution technique that would go on to become fundamentally important to businesses in the Middle Ages. It was even known as The Golden Rule for a time, because of its significance to mercantile trade.

As Ahmes puts it, "A heap and its $^{1}/_{7}$th part become 19. What is the heap?"

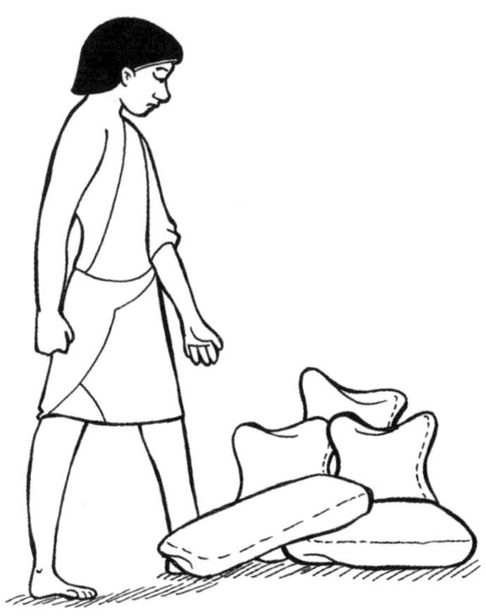

EGYPT
1850BC

SOLUTION PAGE 107

20

PROGRESSIVE SHARES

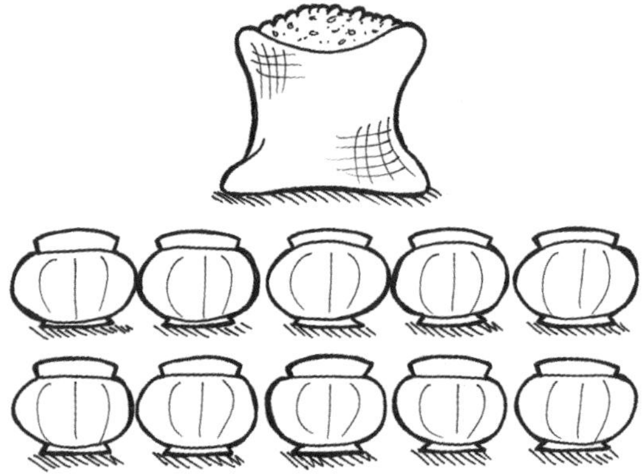

One of Ahmes' more challenging trials involves a rather complex question of mathematical progression – the sort of thing which at one point was thought to have first emerged with the great Greek mathematicians.

In Problem 64 of the *Rhind Papyrus*, he asks:

If it is said to you to divide 10 hekats of barley amongst 10 men, so that the difference of each man to his neighbour in hekats of barley is $^1/_8$th of a hekat, then what is each man's share?

You may make do with finding just the largest share, to save calculating a lot of Egyptian fractions.

EGYPT
1850BC

SOLUTION PAGE 108

SQUARING THE CIRCLE

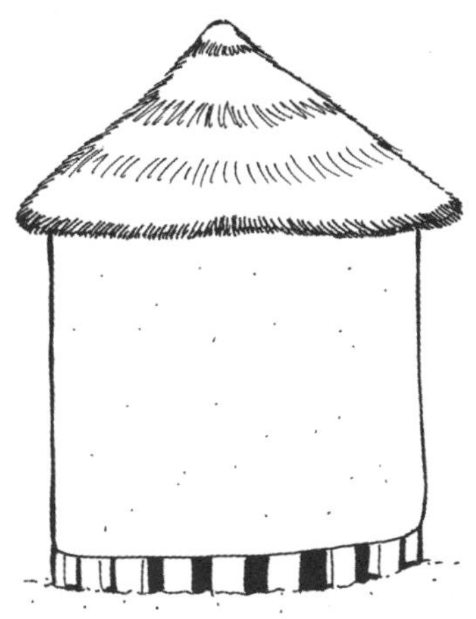

This is one of the *Rhind Papyrus*'s more important puzzles, indicating the understanding of pi as a mathematical constant. Ahmes didn't have an accurate value for pi, but he was clearly aware that there was one, and that it was absolutely fundamental to geometry.

In this puzzle, there is a cylindrical granary of diameter 9 and height 6. How much grain can go into it?

The question assumes that the reader doesn't have any knowledge of pi, so when you're answering this one, you're not allowed to use the standard formula for the area of a circle. Can you work out the answer from first principles?

EGYPT
1850BC

SOLUTION PAGE 108

SQUARE TRIAL

The *Berlin Papyrus* is another ancient Egyptian scroll, one that contains a mixture of medical and mathematical information. It has the earliest known information on pregnancy testing, and is generally classified amongst the Egyptian medical papyri rather than the mathematical ones. It was found early in the 19th century at Saqqara, and like the *Moscow Papyrus*, it is anonymous. It also contains one of the most sophisticated Egyptian *Regula Falsi* problems still extant today.

An area of 100 square cubits is equal to that of two smaller squares together. The side of one is ½ + ¼ the side of the other. What are their sides?

EGYPT
1800BC

SOLUTION PAGE 109

Sumerian Riddle

Sumer, in what is now southern Iraq, is regarded as the cradle of civilization. The nation arose as humans started deliberate intensive cultivation some seven to eight thousand years ago, and the availability of stored food allowed people to move beyond just hunting and gathering to performing social roles that did not directly provide food or defence. Complex records were required to keep all this running, and writing grew out of it as a direct result.

This riddle dates from the last phase of Sumerian history; Sumer would eventually fall, largely thanks to the ecological results of its farming enterprises, to be replaced by Babylon.

There is a house. One enters it blind. One leaves it seeing. What is it?

Sumer
1600BC

Solution page 109

Ramesses' Star

Pharaoh Ramesses II ruled Ancient Egypt at the height of its glory, and had an immense impact on the kingdom. His grandest architectural work was his memorial temple, the Ramesseum at Kurna. It remained an important centre of learning and worship for centuries after his death. The temple was found by modern European scientists at the end of the 18th century. Among the hieroglyphs and decorations, they discovered a curious puzzle painted onto a ceiling – Ramesses' Star. It is one of the oldest puzzles known, and may have been the forerunner of the medieval game of Nine Men's Morris.

The aim is to fill nine of the ten circles on the star with coins, beads, or anything else handy. Place a coin on any empty circle on the star, and jump it over one circle (empty or filled) to another empty circle in a straight line. It is possible to fill nine of the ten circles this way, but it is not easy – if you find yourself getting stuck at six or seven circles, then persevere, and try some lateral thinking.

Egypt
1213BC

Solution page 110

25

THE RIDDLE OF THE SPHINX

The Riddle of the Sphinx is probably the most famous and enduring riddle of them all.

The Sphinx was a monster of ancient Greek myth, the daughter of Typhon and Echidna, with the body of a lion, the head and chest of a woman, a snake in place of a tail, and the wings of an eagle. Although she hailed originally from Ethiopia, she waited in the hills outside the city of Thebes, and demanded that travellers answer her riddle. When they failed to do so correctly, she devoured them. Her question was: "Which creature goes on four legs in the morning, two at mid-day and three in the evening, and the more legs it has, the weaker it is?"

GREECE
800BC

SOLUTION PAGE 110

26

The Quiet One

This is another ancient Greek riddle that has survived since antiquity. As is often the case, it is the universal themes that remain enduring.

What has a mouth but does not speak, what has a bed but never sleeps?

Greece
700BC

Solution page 110

VISITORS

This simple riddle dates back to ancient Greece, and has survived through to the modern day:

At night they come without being called.
By day they are lost without ever leaving.
Who are they?

GREECE
600BC

SOLUTION PAGE 111

CRETANS

Epimenides of Knossos was a Cretan Greek poet, philosopher and visionary in the 6th century BC. In his poem Cretica, he rails against his fellow Cretans for denying the immortality of the god Zeus, saying "The Cretans, always liars, evil beasts". At some point, the poem became associated with the liar paradox, and eventually became known as Epimenides' Paradox.

There is no one formulation of the paradox, but put simply, it says that Epimenides, a Cretan, says "All Cretans are liars." But he himself is a Cretan. If he is telling the truth, his statement has to be a lie, and he is not telling the truth; if he is lying, then he is giving weight to the truth of his statement, and therefore not lying.

What flaws are there in this?

GREECE
550BC

SOLUTION PAGE 111

29

ZENO'S DICHOTOMY

Zeno of Elea was a Greek philosopher who lived from around 490BC to around 430BC, and was placed into a large mortar and pounded to death after taking part in an unsuccessful attempt to overthrow the tyrant Demylus. He was a member of the Eleatic School of philosophy, which held that all existence and time is but one construct, and all appearances to the contrary – plurality, motion, change and so on – are illusory. As a young man, he wrote a book of forty logical paradoxes to support the Eleatic philosophy and bolster his master, Parmenides. Zeno hadn't even decided whether to publish the book or not when it was stolen and published without his permission, and eight of his paradoxes survive, thanks to commentaries by Aristotle and Simplicius. Today, they are his most famous legacy.

In this Dichotomy, also known as Zeno's Racecourse, he points out that movement is impossible because any movement must pass through the half-way stage before it arrives at its goal. But then the half-way stage becomes a new goal, and it too has a half-way, and so on. In fact, even the tiniest movement has an infinity of ever-smaller half-way stages that must be reached first, and no finite amount of time is enough to reach an infinite number of stages.

Ignoring the fact that this is a *reductio ad absurdum* argument that is experimentally obviously wrong – things move – is there a logical flaw here?

GREECE
470BC

SOLUTION PAGE 111

ZENO'S ARROW

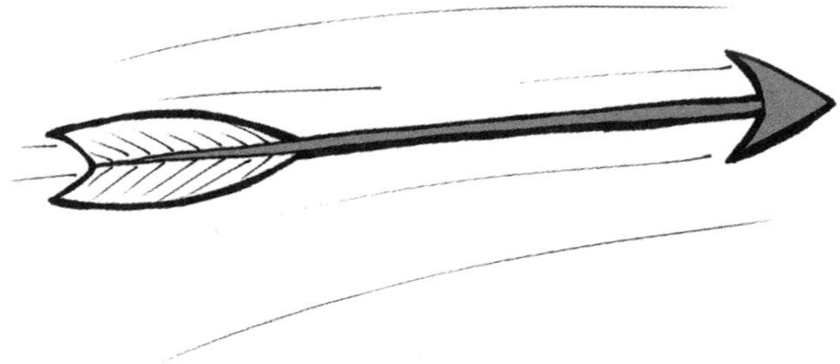

In the Paradox of the Arrow, Zeno points out that an arrow occupies a specific area of space when it is at rest. He then points out that in any given instant, the arrow in flight is at rest. If, during one tiny instant of time, the arrow moved, then it would be possible to divide the instant into before and after moments. Therefore the arrow is motionless, and therefore motion has to be an illusion or, at the very least, to occur between moments somehow, outside of time.

Was he wrong?

GREECE
470BC

SOLUTION PAGE 112

Zeno's Stadium

Another of Zeno's paradoxes of motion is that of the stadium. Imagine that there are two lines of five runners, A and B, running around a track in opposite directions. They are moving at the same speed, as can be clearly observed by a row of five stationary spectators, C. Each row of people is the same length. The two rows of runners cross as they are passing the spectators, A on the outside. The length of A is the same as the length of B and C, and A and B are moving at the same speed. The first member of A will run the entire length of B in x seconds. But B, running at the same speed, will only run half the length of C in the same time. As the lengths of B and C are the same, Zeno asserts that time is x = x*2, which is impossible, and therefore time is illusory.

Is there anything to Zeno's argument?

Greece
470BC

Solution page 112

ACHILLES AND THE TORTOISE

Zeno's most famous paradox is that of Achilles and the Tortoise. In it, he gives a situation where Achilles is in a race with a tortoise, and gives the tortoise a 100m head-start. Once the tortoise reaches 100m, Achilles races to catch up with it. But in the time taken to do so, the tortoise has moved further on. Achilles must catch up to the new point – by which time the tortoise will have moved again. In fact, Achilles will never be able to catch up, because the tortoise will always have moved on by the time he gets to where it had been.

Where's the problem?

GREECE
470BC

SOLUTION PAGE 113

THE HEAP

The Sorites Paradox, named after the Greek word for heap, was coined by Eubulides of Miletus, a Megarian (or Eristic) philosopher from the 4th century BC who spent much of his energy bitterly attacking Aristotle, who was his contemporary. Megarian philosophy, founded by Euclid of Megara, espoused the idea of a single, perfect goodness, a state of grace with similarities to Zeno's Eleatic unity.

Eubulides is known for his paradoxes, most of which arise from setting up situations with vague starting conditions. The Sorites paradox states that a large number of grains of sand collected together is a heap, and taking one grain of sand from it does not stop it being a heap. So is it still a heap when only one grain of sand remains? And if not, when did it switch to not being a heap any more?

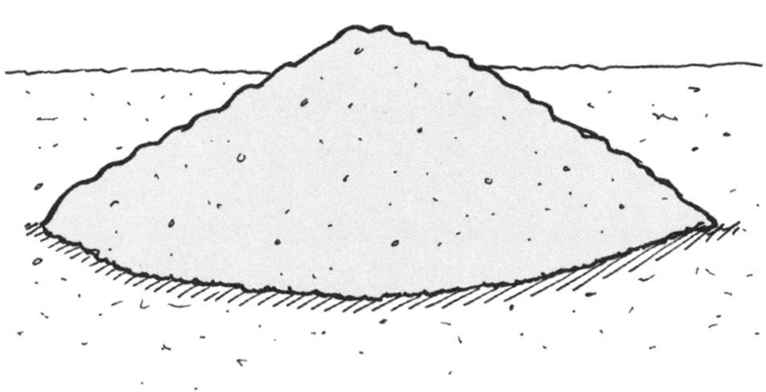

GREECE
440BC

SOLUTION PAGE 113

Four Brothers

This riddle reflects interestingly on ancient Greek thought.

There are four brothers, in this world, who were all born together.
The first brother runs and runs, and never grows tired.
The second brother eats and eats, and is never full.
The third brother drinks and drinks, and is never sated.
The fourth brother sings an unending song, and it is never good.

GREECE
400BC

SOLUTION PAGE 114

THE SHOOT

This short but puzzling riddle comes from ancient Greece:

What has roots that nobody sees,
and towers taller than the trees.
Up, up and up it goes,
Yet day by day it never grows.

GREECE
400BC

SOLUTION PAGE 114

THE NURSERY

This ancient Greek riddle can still stretch modern ingenuity:

There was a green house.
Inside the green house was a white house.
Inside the white house was a red house.
Inside the red house, lots of babies.

GREECE
400BC

SOLUTION PAGE 114

THE LUO RIVER SCROLL

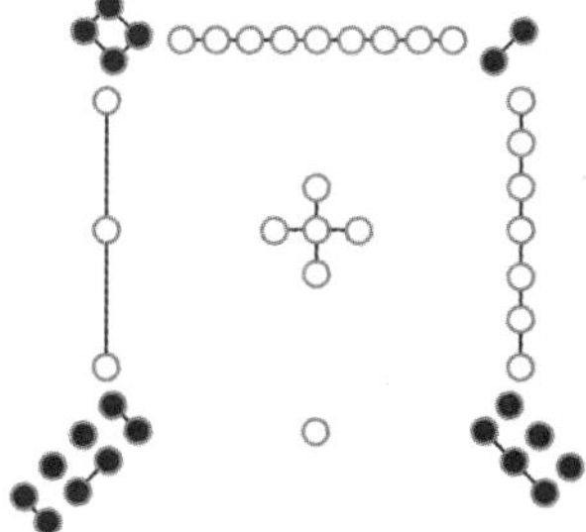

According to legend, China's first emperor was Fu Hsi, half man and half dragon, who consolidated the country into one kingdom around 3000BC. As he was riding along beside the Ho Tu, the Yellow River, one day, he saw a dragon-horse rise from the water, and on it was a curious design, a series of dots set in concentric rings and linked in a particular arrangement. This pattern became known as the Yellow River map, and from it, Fu Hsi derived the eight trigrams of Chinese mystical thought that form the famous divination system of the I Ching, the Book of Changes.

Almost a thousand years later, the Emperor Yu – another legendary figure – was riding beside the Lo Shu, the Luo River, when a tortoise rose from the water, bearing markings similar to the Yellow River map, but in a very different pattern. This pattern became known as the Lo Shu, the Luo River scroll. Yu used it to re-order the eight trigrams, linking them to the five Chinese elements, and it was said that Fu Hsi's arrangement represented the order of things before the world was created, whilst Yu's arrangement represented the order of things in the physical world.

The Lo Shu, shown above, has been captivating and enthralling people all over the world ever since its discovery, although modern scholars put that at around 400BC rather than 2300BC. How is it better known in the West?

CHINA
400BC

SOLUTION PAGE 114

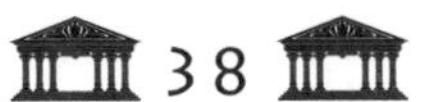

BURIDAN'S ASS

In *De Caelo* (*About the Heavens*), Aristotle discussed the theoretical possibility of a man who is equally hungry and thirsty being poised, equidistant, between food and drink. Unable to decide, he moves to neither, and eventually dies.

French philosopher Jean Buridan, a 14th century thinker, became associated with the problem because he suggested that any fully-informed human when faced with alternative options will always choose the one that leads to the greatest good, after due consideration. Later philosophers used Aristotle's thoughts to satirise Buridan, suggesting that an ass placed between two equally tempting bales of hay would starve trying to decide which to eat.

One common response to the paradox is to point out that sometimes an arbitrary decision is perfectly rational, and that it is much more rational just to pick one rather than starve. Can you think of another response?

GREECE
340BC

SOLUTION PAGE 115

39

Hui Shi's Third Paradox

The Chinese philosopher Hui Shi lived some time around the start of the 3rd century BC, during China's Warring States period. He was famous as a rhetorician, devoting himself to a doctrine that argued the arbitrary nature of human perception, and the consequent need to treat all of nature benevolently. He left a set of ten famous paradoxes, some of which are not so much paradoxical as statements of philosophy.

In Hui Shi's third paradox, he states that "Heaven is as low as earth, mountains are level with marshes."

What is he getting at?

China
300BC

Solution page 115

THE LADDER OF HORUS

The right-angled triangle has been one of the most prevalent and fundamental mathematical discoveries in human history. It allows the reliable construction of square angles, which in turn permits advances in construction, manufacturing and a host of other areas. The most common version found in history is the poster-boy for Pythagoras' theorem, the 3-4-5 triangle.

The Egyptians had early knowledge of the importance of right-angled triangles, with particular emphasis on the 3-4-5. It was said that the length 3 section belonged to Isis, the length 4 section to Osiris, and the length 5 hypotenuse to their son, the hawk-headed god Horus.

The earliest clear use of the triangle as an Egyptian puzzle appears around 300BC. The problem it asks is trivial to us, of course: "If a ladder of 10 cubits has its base 6 cubits from a wall, how high will it reach?" The answer is a simple doubling of the Pythagorean triple of 3-4-5.

A more interesting question is about Pythagorean triples themselves, which consist of three integers that could describe the sides of a right-angled triangle. Discounting any simple multiples of other triples, how many triples are there with a hypotenuse of less than 20?

EGYPT
300BC

SOLUTION PAGE 115

THE ZERO PROOF

There are a number of places where common mathematical assumptions break down, and provide scope for seemingly paradoxical proofs. Euclid collected together an entire volume of such falsities, to help show the importance of rigour in mathematical thought. It is reasonably straightforward to show that 0 = 1, and by extension, that maths is flawed.

Start by adding an infinite number of zeros together. No matter how much nothing you add, you still have nothing. 0 = 0 + 0 + 0 + 0 + 0 +...

Now, 1 - 1 is 0, so you can just as easily read that as 0 = (1 -1) + (1 -1) + (1 -1) +...

But if that is true – and it is – the associative law states that you can bracket the sums as you like, so long as you don't change the order of any digits, so 0 = 1 (-1 +1) + (-1 +1) + (-1 +1) +...

As (-1 + 1) is 0, this becomes 0 = 1 + 0 + 0 + 0 +...

And 0 = 1.

What's the error?

GREECE
300BC

SOLUTION PAGE 116

Crocodile Tears

An ancient Greek paradox of uncertain authorship involved a hungry crocodile snatching a baby from its mother on the banks of the Nile. The mother begged for mercy, and the crocodile wanted to look good in the eyes of the gods, and so agreed to give her a chance to win her baby back. The crocodile told her, "If you correctly predict the fate of your baby, then I will return him. Otherwise, I will eat him."

Given that the crocodile wants to eat the baby, is there anything that the mother can say to get her child back?

Greece
300BC

Solution page 116

43

The Sieve of Eratosthenes

	2	3		5		7			
11		13				17		19	
		23						29	
31						37			
41		43				47			
		53						59	
61						67			
71		73						79	
		83						89	
						97			

Prime numbers, being indivisible, are one of the most fundamental mathematical concepts, and, like square numbers, have often been the source of mystical speculation. The ancient Greeks were particularly sophisticated in their handling of prime numbers. The Greek mathematical master Euclid proved that there must be an infinite number of primes.

You can use Euclid's method to discover new primes, with patience, but you can't be sure of catching all of them that way. You can also use even more patience and, for each number, check if it can be divided by the other primes you already know to discover if it is prime. If you get past its square root without finding a prime divisor, your target number is prime. You'll get them all, but while that's OK for small numbers, it's horribly time-consuming for larger ones.

Eratosthenes, an approximate contemporary of Euclid's from the 3rd century BC, devised a brilliantly simple way of making it quicker to find prime numbers, and it became known as his Sieve, for the patterns it made. Given the technique's name, can you work out what the method is?

Greece
250BC

Solution page 117

Archimedes' Revenge

Archimedes of Syracuse was a Greek scientist who died in 212 BC at the age of 75. He is remembered as one of the greatest mathematicians of all time, and possibly the greatest scientist of the ancient world. It is said that he devised the most fiendishly difficult puzzle of all, created as a challenge and rebuke to Apollonius of Perga, a geometrician who had suggested improvements to some of Archimedes' theorems. Archimedes' Revenge was then supposedly sent to Eratosthenes, the chief librarian at the legendary Great Library of Alexandria, for the library staff to work on.

The challenge is to calculate the numbers of the cattle of the sun, belonging to the gods. There were four different herds, one white, one black, one yellow and one dappled. The number of white bulls was equal to a half plus a third of the black bulls, plus all of the yellow bulls. The black bulls were equal to a quarter of the dappled plus a fifth, plus all of the yellow ones. The dappled bulls were equal to one sixth of the white plus one seventh, plus all the yellow ones. The number of white cows was equal to one third plus a quarter of the entire black herd. The black cows were equal to a quarter of the dappled herd plus a fifth. A quarter of the dappled cows were equal to a fifth plus a sixth of the yellow herd. The yellow cows were equal to a sixth plus a seventh of the white herd. When the white and black herds mingled, their combined number was a perfect square. Similarly, when the dappled and yellow herds mingled, they came to a triangular number. How many cows and bulls were there in each herd?

Be warned: many professional mathematicians would need either a high-powered computer or several years of hard work to solve this puzzle.

Greece
230BC

Solution page 118

THE NINE CHAPTERS

The Nine Chapters on the Mathematical Art is a collection of mathematical teachings from early China. The book was known in 179AD, and may actually be several centuries earlier; its most important commentary, written in 263AD by mathematician Liu Hui, credits Zhang Cang, who died in 142BC, as the work's earliest compiler. The actual original authors are anonymous, but the book illuminated and shaped mathematical thought in the East until at least the 1600s.

One of the book's most important concepts is that of abstract numeration. Concrete numeration is obvious to anyone – one apple is one apple, both three grapes and three plums are groups of 3, and so on. The natural numbers are just that, natural. Abstract numbers are far harder to grasp if you don't already know them. The *Nine Chapters* contains problems which require the use of both 0 and negative numbers to solve. Both of these are extremely counter-intuitive, and require that you think of absence as somehow a concrete, solid thing.

This puzzle is from the eighth chapter, "Fang Cheng".

There are three grades of corn, each of which comes in a basket of a particular size. Two baskets of first-grade corn do not make one measure, and neither do three baskets of second-grade corn, nor four baskets of third-grade corn. However, if you add one basket of second-grade to the two first-grade baskets, or one basket of third-grade to the three second-grade baskets, or one basket of first-grade to the four third-grade baskets, then you would have one measure in each case. What proportion of a measure does each basket size contain?

CHINA
150BC

SOLUTION PAGE 119

46

THE CISTERN PROBLEM

The cistern problem dates back to the *Nine Chapters*, and is part of a common thread of puzzle challenges that crops up regularly in civilisations all over the world. This is probably because the premise is both practical and fairly fundamental.

There is a cistern of volume 48 which has two inlet taps and one outlet tap. The first inlet tap alone will fill the cistern in 12 hours. The second alone will fill it in 6 hours. The third alone will empty it in 8 hours. If the cistern is emptied and all three taps are opened, how many hours will it take for it to fill up?

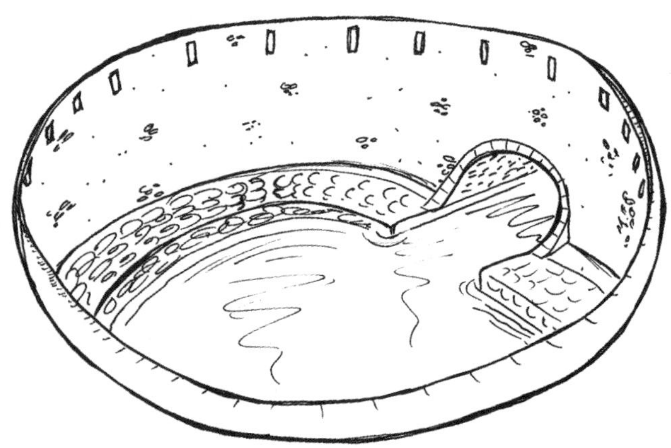

CHINA
150BC

SOLUTION PAGE 120

DOG AND HARE

The sixth chapter of the *The Nine Chapters on the Mathematical Art* deals with the mathematical knowledge required for purposes of taxation – how to distribute taxes, transport grain, and so on. This section also introduced pursuit problems, where the puzzle involves working out how soon a pursuing party will catch up with a fleeing one. The possible implications of this inclusion are left to the reader.

This puzzle states that a fleeing hare and a chasing dog are 50pu apart. The dog will catch the hare after a chase of 125pu. How much longer will the chase be once the dog has closed to a distance of 30pu?

CHINA
150BC

SOLUTION PAGE 120

48

THE CHICKENS

The seventh chapter of the *The Nine Chapters on the Mathematical Art* is devoted to what the authors called 'Excess and Deficiency' problems – the same sort of *Regula Falsi* approach that Ahmes made use of in the *Rhind Papyrus*. In the Chinese method, two answers were usually given, one greater and one lesser than the actual answer required, which is where the technique drew its name from.

In this puzzle, a group of people are buying a consignment of chickens from a stall, and they are each paying the same amount of money. If they each contribute 9 wen, they are paying 11 wen too much, and if they contribute 6 wen, then are paying 16 too little.

How many people are there, and what is the cost of the consignment?

CHINA
150BC

SOLUTION PAGE 120

LEG AND THIGH

The entire ninth chapter of *The Nine Chapters on the Mathematical Art* is about right-angled triangles, possibly because they were so critical in accurately assessing land distribution for farming. The chapter is named Kou Ku, a term derived from the names given to the sides of a right-angled triangle. The two sides that formed the right-angle on a right-angled triangle were named Kou and Ku, Leg and Thigh. The hypotenuse, stretching between the two tips, was known as the Hsien, or lute-string.

This puzzle is concerned with discovering the size of the largest square that can fit inside a right-angle triangle, making use of the pre-existing right-angle in its construction.

There is a right-angled triangle with Kou of 5 ch'ih, and Ku of 12 ch'ih. How many ch'ih is the largest square that can fit inside?

CHINA
150BC

SOLUTION PAGE 121

Men Buy a Horse

The *Nine Chapters* also features the first known instance of the Men Buy a Horse puzzle, a commonly-encountered type of problem.

There are three men who are considering buying a horse that costs 24 yuan. Individually, none of the three has enough money. The first man says, "If I borrowed a half of the money that you two have, I could buy the horse." The second man says, "If I borrowed two thirds of the money that you two have, I could buy the horse and still have around half a yuan left." The third man says, "Well, if I borrowed three quarters of the money that you two have, I could buy the horse and still have one and a half yuan left over."

Assuming each man has a whole number of yuan, how much does each man have?

China
150BC

Solution page 121

GREED

This Ancient Greek puzzle is somewhat more abstract than it appears at first blush:

The more of them you take for yourself, the more of them you leave behind for others.

What are they?

GREECE
100BC

SOLUTION PAGE 121

Posthumous Twins

The Posthumous Twins problem arose when Roman law decreed that the legal heir of an estate should receive at least 1/4 of that estate, and if the will was invalidated, only the deceased's children could inherit. The idea was to cement the rights of the eldest son of the deceased with respect to a possible widow or other claimant.

In this problem, a dying man with a pregnant wife makes a will which states that if his wife has a male child, the son should get ⅔ of the estate and the wife should get ⅓. If she has a female child, the wife will get the larger ⅔ share, and the daughter will get ⅓. After the man's death, the wife gives birth to twins, one boy and one girl.

How is the estate to be shared?

Rome
50BC

Solution page 122

THE SHIP OF THESEUS

Plutarch was a Greek-born philosopher and historian who lived in the 1st century AD. He is best known now for his book *Parallel Lives*, a series of 23 biographical studies of historical figures, arranged in pairs, one Greek, one Roman. He looked at character, in particular, and drew interesting correspondences between his pairs.

In a piece on the Greek hero Theseus, Plutarch notes that on his return to Athens, the ship that he had travelled in was preserved as a historic relic. As the planks decayed, the old timbers were removed, and replaced with lovingly-crafted exact duplicates. In this manner, the ship was preserved down through the centuries, even to the 3rd century BC.

The question Plutarch poses is, if all of the pieces of wood that make up the ship have been replaced, possibly many times, is it still the same ship?

ROME
100AD

SOLUTION PAGE 122

Men Find a Purse

The Men Find a Purse problem has been cropping up regularly in different mathematically-inclined cultures since its first appearance in ancient Greece. In his masterwork *Liber Abaci,* published in 1202, Fibonacci devotes an entire section of the book to discussion of the problem and various different versions of it.

Three men were walking together when they discovered a purse of money. They examine the purse, and the first says to the second, "If I took this purse, I would have twice as much money as you." The second says to the third, "I would have three times as much as you." The third says to the first "I would have four times as much as you." How much does the purse hold, and how much does each man have?

Greece
250AD

Solution page 123

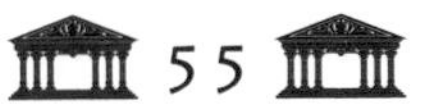

THE UNWANTED

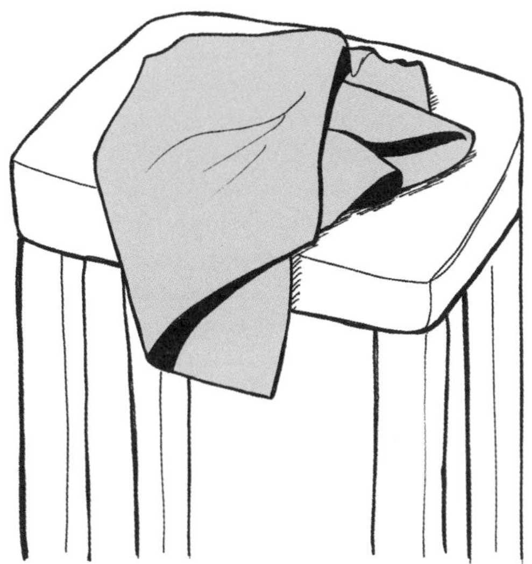

This is a rather telling riddle from Roman times:

He who has it does not say it.
He who takes it does not know it.
He who knows it does not want it.
Yet, men die for it.
What is it?

ROME
300AD

SOLUTION PAGE 123

THE FIVE SONS

It was an Arabic puzzle which took the idea of even distribution of varied resources to a pinnacle of complex challenge. Its history is uncertain, but it appeared in several volumes of Arabic puzzle collections in the second half of the last millennium, and may have been considerably older than that.

In this puzzle, a dying father leaves a range of wine casks to his five sons. His bequest amounts to 45 casks in total, 9 holding 4 pints, 9 holding 3 pints, 9 holding 2 pints, 9 holding 1 pint, and 9 containing nothing. The wine is to be shared equally, in both amount of wine (18 pints) and number of casks (9). Each son wants to get at least one of each cask, and each of them wants to receive a different distribution of casks to any of their brothers.

How can this be done?

ARABIA
400AD

SOLUTION PAGE 124

SUN TZU'S CLASSIC PROBLEM

In the book *Sun Tzu Suanjing*, 3rd century AD Chinese mathematician Sun Tzu – a different person to the world-famous military general, who lived some five centuries earlier – introduced an important principle in number theory, known now as the Chinese Remainder Theorem. His illustrative question for the Theorem has become known as Sun Tzu's Classic Problem.

We have a group of things of which we do not know the number. If we count them by threes, the remainder is two. If we count them by fives, the remainder is 3. If we count them by sevens, the remainder is two. How many things are there?

CHINA
400AD

SOLUTION PAGE 124

The Trouble with Camels

A traditional Arabic puzzle, most likely owing its conception to the ancient Egyptian style of fractional representation, specifies that in an old Arabian city, a wealthy merchant died and, in his will, left specific instructions regarding the disposition of his livestock. His lawyer met the merchant's three sons, and explained to them that his father had insisted that his eldest son receive a full half of his camels. The middle son was to get a third of the herd, and his youngest son, still with plenty of time to make his fortunes, was to get just one ninth.

Unfortunately, the herd consisted of 17 camels, and the brothers could see no way to honour their father's wishes without killing at least one of the beasts and chopping it into chunks. The lawyer, however, had a better idea. Without any loss to himself, and without involving a fifth party, he was able to show the brothers how the herd could be divided equally, keeping all the camels alive.

How did he do it?

Arabia
400AD

Solution page 125

THE SNAIL AND THE WELL

The Snail and the Well puzzle first appeared in India, with the great Jain mathematicians. Its earliest appearance dates to some time after the work of the celebrated 7th century mathematicians Bhaskara and Brahmagupta.

A snail is at the bottom of a well 4½ feet deep. On the first day it climbs two feet, and then slips back down one foot during the night. It is getting tired however, and so each subsequent day, it climbs 10% less that it did the day before. It always slips down the same one foot at night. Will the snail ever get out of the well, and if so, when?

INDIA
700AD

SOLUTION PAGE 125

60

Alcuin's Camel

Alcuin of York was a religious scholar and teacher in Dark Age Europe. He was a student at the great school of York, which was founded in 627AD by St. Paulinus of York. The school, now called St. Peter's, is the world's fifth-oldest school. Some time around 750 AD, Alcuin assumed a teaching role at the school, and became headmaster in 767 AD. As well as the obvious religious studies, the school taught the liberal arts and sciences, which included logic and mathematical subjects.

Alcuin of York is thought to be the author of the *Propositiones ad Acuendes Juvenes* (*Propositions for Sharpening Youths*), one of the first books of puzzles collected for teaching or recreation. The oldest surviving copy dates to the end of the 9th century.

One of Alcuin of York's better known puzzles from the *Propositiones* is an early example of what is now known as the jeep problem. A certain head of a household ordered that 90 modia of grain be taken from one of his houses to another, 30 leagues away. Given that this load must be carried in three trips (the camel can manage 30 modia as a maximum load), and that the camel must eat one modius per league, how many modia can be left over at the end of the journey?

ENGLAND
770AD

SOLUTION PAGE 126

61

Brothers and Sisters

Several of Alcuin of York's problems remain popular and influential today in one form or another. Possibly the best known of these is this puzzle, where three brother and sister pairs need to get across a river in a small boat, but to stop the men's lust overcoming them, a woman may only be in the presence of a man if he is her brother, or if her brother is present.

There were three men, each having an unmarried sister, who needed to cross a river. Each man was desirous of his friends' sisters. Coming to the river, they found only a small boat in which only two persons could cross at a time. Let them say, they who are able, how did they cross the river, so that none of the sisters were defiled by the men?

Given the dubious assumption that all men would be happy to rape their friends' sisters given a moment's chance, the best solution takes 11 crossings.

What is the process?

England
770AD

Solution page 126

62

Alcuin's Flasks

In this puzzle, Proposition 12, Alcuin of York describes a situation where flasks containing three different volumes of oil are to be divided equally among three sons so that each gets the same.

A father dies and leaves his three sons 30 flasks. 10 of these are full of oil, 10 are half-full, and 10 are empty. Divide the oil and flasks so that an equal share of both comes to each son.

All well and good. But is it possible to do this so that each son gets a different distribution of flasks to the other two, and each son gets at least one of each type of flask?

England
770AD

Solution page 127

63

The Eastern Merchant

Another of Alcuin of York's problems asks the reader to solve a problem of indeterminacy. A certain merchant in the East wished to buy 100 assorted animals for 100 solidi. He ordered his servant to pay five solidi per camel, one solidus per ass, and one solidus per 20 sheep, and to get at least one of each. Let them say, they who wish, how many camels, asses and sheep were obtained for 100 solidi?

England
770AD

Solution page 127

64

Alcuin's Grain

This is Proposition 32, Concerning the Head of a Certain Household. Alcuin of York gives a distribution problem as a way of encouraging his students to work around issues of indeterminate conditions. He actually gives several such problems, varying mainly in the amount of grain, which rather reinforces that he wanted the students to learn the knack of solving problems of this sort.

A head of a certain household has 20 servants. He ordered them to be given 20 modia of corn as follows: the men should receive 3 modia, the women 2 modia, and the children, half a modium. Let them say, they who can, how many men, women and children must there have been.

You should assume that there is at least one of each.

England
770AD

Solution page 128

65

The Hundred Steps

Alcuin of York's 42nd Proposition, Concerning the Ladder Having 100 Steps, was famously given to a young Johann Gauss, a German scientist who remains known as one of the most influential mathematical figures in history. Gauss was only seven at the time, which dates the event to 1784 AD. It is said that by the time the teacher had finished instructing the class in the problem, Gauss had the solution.

There is a ladder which has 100 steps. One dove sat on the first step, two doves on the second, three on the third, four on the fourth, five on the fifth, and so on up to the hundredth step. How many doves were there in all?

England
770AD

Solution page 128

Alcuin's Riddle

In 781AD, Alcuin was reluctantly poached away from York by the Emperor Charlemagne, to revitalise the school at his court. In this latter role, he educated many of Europe's leading nobles, scholars and ecclesiasts, training them in the liberal arts and sciences, and becoming friendly with most of them.

Alcuin posed the following riddle to the Archbishop Ridulf of Mainz, known as Damoeta, in return for a gift:

A beast has sudden come to this my house,
A beast of wonder, who two heads has got,
And yet the beast has only one jaw-bone.
Twice three times ten of horrid teeth it has.
Its food grows always on this body of mine,
Not flesh, fruit. It eats not with its teeth,
Drinks not. Its open mouth shows no decay.
Tell me, Damoeta dear, what beast is this?

Ridulf had the advantage of knowing what gift he had just sent Alcuin. Can you identify the 'beast' without that inside knowledge?

England
780AD

Solution page 129

67 The Josephus Problem

Titus Flavius Josephus was a Jewish war-leader during the first Jewish-Roman war, 66–73AD. He was captured by the Romans in 67AD, and persuaded to work as a negotiator for them. He documented the fall of Jerusalem in 70AD, and became a Roman historian shortly afterwards.

During his capture, Josephus says that he found himself trapped in a cave with 40 companions. The Romans asked him to surrender, but his men refused to allow it, opting instead for collective suicide. They formed a circle and killed each other one by one, killing the third man each time and closing the circle's ranks. By claimed happenstance, Josephus was in the correct place to be the last man alive, and he persuaded the man before him, the second to last, to surrender with him.

This historical event became the object of mathematical speculation, first appearing as a puzzle in an Irish text from around 800AD. If Josephus started in position number 31 in the circle of 41, where would his surviving compatriot have been?

Ireland
800AD

Solution page 129

68

The Explorer's Problem

The original version of The Explorer's Problem originates with Alcuin, and his camels, in the 8th century AD. This problem departs somewhat from Alcuin's original question, but provides an interesting counterpoint to it.

An explorer in the desert wishes to arrive at an oasis as darkness is falling, so that he does not have to sit around in the heat, nor will he risk missing the oasis in the darkness. From his current position, if he rides at 10 miles an hour, he will arrive an hour after darkness has fallen. If he rides at 15 miles an hour, he will arrive an hour too soon, and swelter. At what speed should he ride to reach the oasis at sunset?

United Kingdom
800AD

Solution page 129

69 Monkey Nuts

A highly influential 9th century Indian mathematician, Mahaveeracharya, established the impossibility of discovering the square root of a negative number, described a method for discovering lowest common multiples, made several key advances in geometry, and disentangled mathematics and astrology, setting the ground for Indian mathematics – already sophisticated – to develop even further.

In his 850AD treatise *Ganit Saar Sangraha*, the *Mathematical Digest*, Mahaveera posed this question which still regularly appears in puzzle compendiums and newspaper entertainment pages today.

Three sailors and their pet monkey find themselves shipwrecked on a small desert island. They immediately set to gathering a pile of coconuts, and when darkness falls, they decide to divide the coconuts in the morning. During the night however, one sailor awakes and decides to take his third early. He divides the pile into threes, with one coconut left over, which he gives to the monkey. He then hides his third, and piles the remaining coconuts back together again. Later, another sailor awakes and does exactly the same, again finding that when he divides the pile into three, there is one coconut left to give to the monkey. Finally the third sailor follows suit, again with one coconut left for the monkey. In the morning, the sailors awake, and agreeably divide the pile of coconuts remaining into three. Once more, there is one left over, which they give to the monkey.

What is the least number of coconuts that there could have been to begin with?

India
850AD

Solution page 130

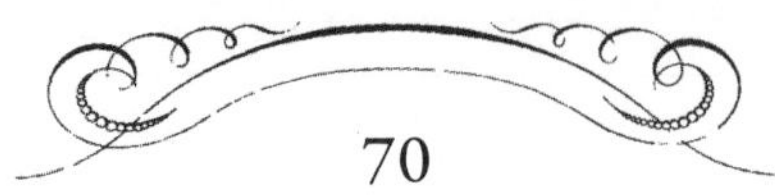

70

THE BOOK OF PRECIOUS THINGS

Abu Kamil, an Egyptian mathematician who lived between 850 and 930AD, was a dedicated algebraist who earned himself the nickname al-Hasib al-Misri, "the Egyptian Calculator". In his *Book of Precious Things in the Art of Reckoning*, he laments the fact that many puzzles have multiple possible answers, and people tend not to realize this. He gives the example of this puzzle, which proves to have far more answers than generally recognized.

It is a reasonably straightforward indeterminate problem: you must buy 100 birds using exactly 100 drachmas. Ducks cost 2 drachmas each, Hens are 1 drachma, a dove is ½ drachma, a ringdove is ⅓ drachma, and a lark is ¼ drachma. You need to buy at least one of each. How many of each do you buy?

It's not too tricky to get an answer for. If you want a real challenge though, also work out how many possible solutions there are.

EGYPT
890AD

SOLUTION PAGE 130

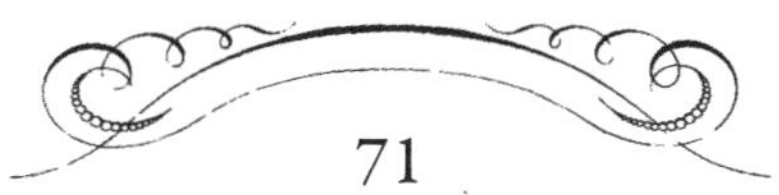

A Medieval Riddle

Leofric, the first bishop of Exeter, assumed his lofty position in 1050AD. Among other acts, he donated a large book of poems and riddles to the cathedral library. The *Exeter Book*, as it is now known, is the largest surviving collection of Old English literature. The author or compiler is unknown, but the date of its creation is thought to have been in the second half of the 10th century. Riddle 25 of the *Exeter Book* has become well-known. See what you make of it.

"I am a wondrous creature: to women a thing of desire; to neighbours serviceable. I harm no city-dweller, except my slayer alone. My stalk is erect and tall – I stand up in bed – and shaggy down below (I won't say where). Sometimes a countryman's comely daughter will venture, proud girl, to get a grip on me. She assaults my redness, plunders my head, and fixes me in a tight place. The one who afflicts me so, this woman with curly locks, will soon feel the effect of her encounter with me – an eye will be wet."

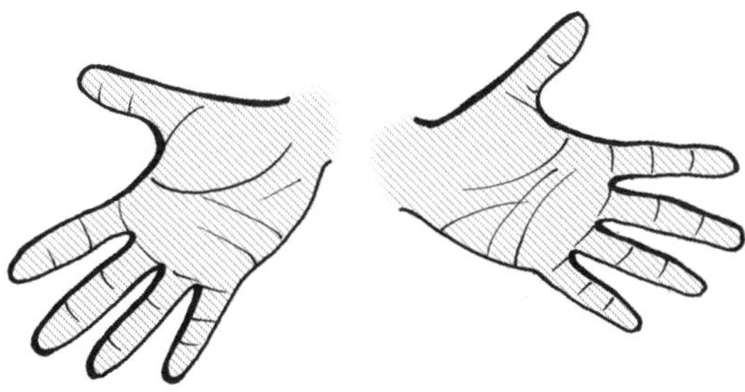

England
950AD

Solution page 131

72

The Mariner

This interesting riddle is found in the *Exeter Book*, Leofric's gift to Exeter Cathedral library on his assumption in 1050AD.

> Often I must war with waves, fight the wind –
> Strive with both at the same time – when I depart to seek
> the earth beneath the waters. To me, my home is alien.
> If I am strong in the struggle, if I can hold my ground.
> Should I fall back, even a little, my foes are stronger,
> and, wrenching me away, soon force me to flee,
> stealing away the treasure that I must keep safe.
> I will forbid this so long as my tail endures,
> and the stones have power against my strength.
> What am I called?

England
950AD

Solution page 131

73

The Memory Wheel

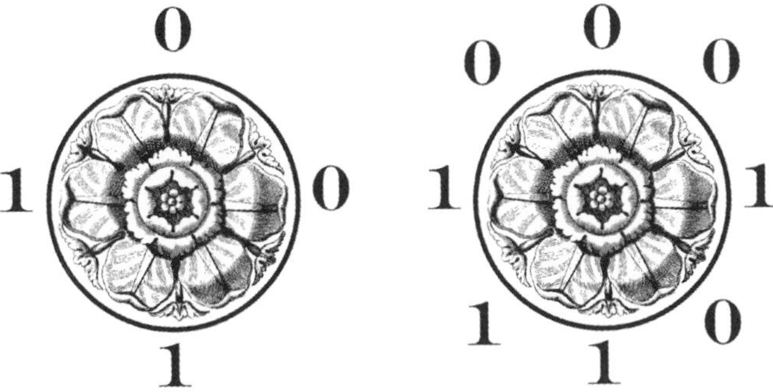

The images shown here are simple examples of memory wheels, used in such disparate settings as Sanskrit poetry, telegraph communication, probability theory and even some older computing applications. In fact, the larger of the two wheels is intrinsically linked to the Sanskrit sutra "YamAtArAjabhAnasalagAm", which is first thought to have appeared around 1000AD.

How are the wheels used, and how do they link to the YamAtArAjabhAnasalagAm?

India
1000AD

Solution page 131

74

Jia Xian's Triangle

Travelling mathematics teacher Zhu Shijie was one of the greatest Chinese mathematicians of the middle ages era. Two of his books have made it through to modern times, the 1299AD *Introduction to Computational Studies*, and 1303's *Jade Mirror of the Four Unknowns*. The former work was an introductory textbook on maths, algebra and geometry that shaped mathematical development in the region for centuries. The *Jade Mirror* was significantly more important however, pushing back the boundaries of algebraic thought at the time.

Amongst the other techniques and innovations in the *Jade Mirror*, Shijie documented a mathematical tool known as Jia Xian's Triangle, used to solve complex polynomial equations. The Triangle dated back to around 1050AD, first appearing in a work called *Shi Suo Suan Shu* by the mathematician Jia Xian. The Triangle predates several important European mathematical discoveries, and its first discovery may have been as early as 500BC in India.

How is it derived and, in the West, better known?

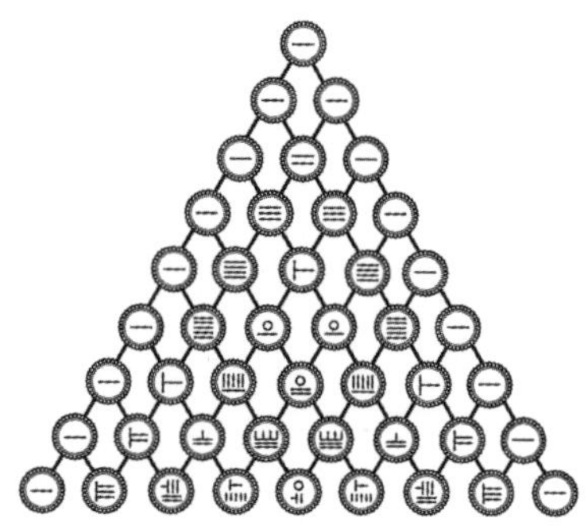

China
1050AD

Solution page 132

75

The Old One

Riddles have been an important part of oral cultures worldwide for centuries. Try this one:

> Though I'm of great age,
> I'm held in a cage,
> And have a long tail and one ear.
> My mouth it is round,
> And when joys abound,
> Oh, then I sing beautiful clear.

United Kingdom
1200AD

Solution page 132

The Trouble with Rabbits

This is a simple, well-known puzzle, but it has its genesis in 13th century Italy, and its implications have been profound for both mathematics and the natural sciences.

Assume that there is a pair of mature rabbits at a certain place, entirely surrounded by a wall. The nature of these rabbits is such that they breed another pair every month, and that the newcomers themselves reach maturity and begin to breed in the second month after their birth.

How many pairs of rabbits can be bred from this pair in one year?

Italy
1202AD

Solution page 132

77

The Ring Game

In 1202, Leonardo of Pisa introduced the Hindu-Arabic number system to Europe in his book *Liber Abaci*, the *Book of Calculation*. Fibonacci, as he is now usually known, travelled around southern Europe and north Africa studying with the greatest Arab mathematicians of the time, and became one of the greatest mathematical minds of the Middle Ages.

Liber Abaci explained the decimal system, gave clear instructions on multiplication and fractions, and showed how the Hindu-Arabic system related to the full range of commercial transactions – and, more to the point, how it made them much simpler than with Roman numerals. It had a huge effect on European thought, and paved the way for the Renaissance, and the growth of European culture

In the *Liber Abaci*, Fibonacci describes a game which mathematically adept hosts can use to impress and confound their guests. The guests sit in a line, and one of them chooses a ring he or she is wearing. This person takes their position in the line, doubles it, adds 5, multiplies by 5, and then adds 10 to this total. Then the number of the ring-finger across the two hands is counted and added, and the value is multiplied by 10. Finally, a number for the knuckle joint is added on. Obviously, both hosts and guests have to agree on the numbering in advance! "When this number is announced," as Fibonacci says, "it is easy to pinpoint the ring."

How?

Italy
1202AD

Solution page 133

The Well

In the *Liber Abaci*, Fibonacci introduced the Well Between Two Towers problem: There are two towers, the heights of which are 40 paces and 30 paces. They are 50 paces apart, and between the two towers is a well. Two birds, sitting atop the two separate towers, take wing at the same instant, and fly at the same speed directly to the well. They arrive there at the same time. What distance is the well from the higher tower?

Italy
1202AD

Solution page 133

79

Tartaglia's Wine

Niccolo Fontana was a 16th century Venetian mathematician and engineer. He became known as Tartaglia, "The Stammerer", after receiving a savage wound to his mouth and tongue during the French massacre of his birth-town of Brescia. He was just twelve. Essentially self-taught, Tartaglia went on to publish a host of books, including very important translations of Euclid and Archimedes.

In his works, Tartaglia published a measuring puzzle that first appeared in the writings of the Abbot of the Convent of the Blessed Virgin Mary, in Stade, near Hamburg, around 1240. The puzzle remains well-known and popular today.

You have three jugs which can hold 8, 5 and 3 pints of wine respectively. The largest one is full, and the other two are empty. Without spilling any wine, or using any other tools, it is possible to end up with two equal four-pint portions.

How?

Germany
1240AD

Solution page 134

80

Topsy-Turvy

This traditional English riddle looks simple until you think about it:
What is it that walks all day on its head?

England
1300AD

Solution page 134

81
The Wanderer

This traditional English riddle has been around since the medieval period at least:

> Old Mother Twitchett had just one eye,
> And a dangling tail which she let fly.
> Every time she leaped over a gap,
> She caught a bit of her tail in a trap.

England
1400AD

Solution page 134

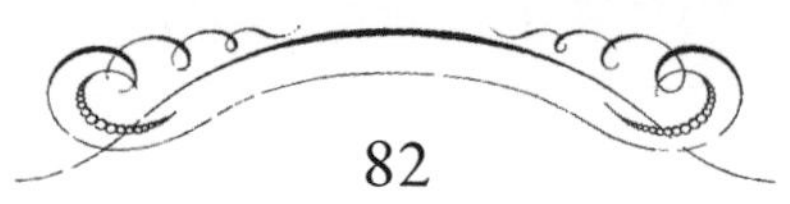

The Hound

An interesting traditional riddle from medieval Germany:

I run through woods and fields all day,
Sit under the bed at night in company,
With my long tongue hanging out,
Waiting only to be fed.

Germany
1450AD

Solution page 135

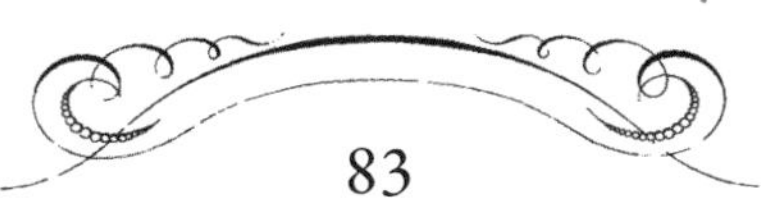

Regiomontanus Angle

The 15th century German astrologer and mathematician Regiomontanus was a celebrated scholar even in his own lifetime. He was said to have fashioned an eagle made of wood which was able to fly from the city under its own power, meet and salute the emperor, and return again. His interest in astrology and astronomy gave him great insight into trigonometric mathematics, and Copernicus considered him an influential inspiration. Regiomontanus' angle problem was devised to reinforce certain geometric principles.

Suppose there is a painting hanging from a wall, its base above eye level. If one stands too far away, the painting appears small. If one stands too close, it is foreshortened. In fact, there is just one point at which the viewer gets the maximum exposure to the painting, the place which maximises the angle formed between the top of the frame, the viewer's eyes and the bottom of the frame.

Where is it?

Germany
1460AD

Solution page 135

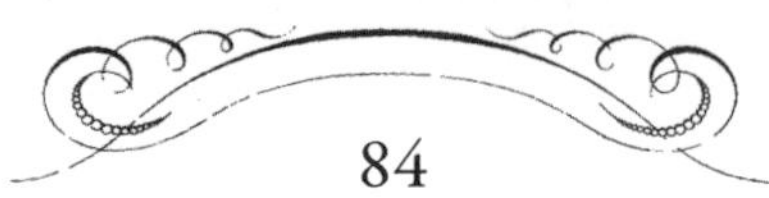

The Problem of Points

The issue of the Problem of Points dates to a hypothetical situation posited by Fra. Luca Pacioli, an Italian mathematician and priest, in 1494. Pacioli described a game in which two players were competing. Each had an equal chance of winning any given round, and agreed in advance that the overall winner of X many rounds would collect the prize.

But what happens if the game is interrupted before it is finished? How could the players divide the pot fairly, taking into account the state of play at the time?

Italy
1494AD

Solution page 135

MODESTY

English tradition has this riddle to offer:

I am within as white as snow,
Without as green as herbs that grow;
I am higher than a house,
and yet am lesser than a mouse.

ENGLAND
1500AD

SOLUTION PAGE 136

86

Dürer's Square

Albrecht Dürer, who died in 1528 aged 56, was an artist at the centre of the Renaissance in Europe, and was instrumental in helping its spread into Germany and the rest of northern Europe. He helped establish woodcuts as an art form, was one of the first landscape painters, and produced vitally important works on artistic theory.

One of Dürer's greatest works is an allegorical engraving titled *Melencolia I*. The piece is laden with symbolism and hidden meaning, and remains one of the most hotly-debated and analysed prints today. In *Melencolia I*, a most incredible Magic Square hangs on the wall behind the main figure. In it, the rows, columns and diagonals all add to 34, and the two numbers at bottom centre are also the date of the engraving, 1514. There are a number of surprising symmetries if you square all the numbers too, and more besides than we have scope to discuss here.

Consider just the number of different ways that this square can be divided into four groups of four numbers, using all the numbers in the square just once, so that each of the groups sums to 34. How many are there – including rows, columns and diagonals/off-diagonals?

16	3	2	13
5	10	11	8
9	6	7	12
4	15	14	1

Germany
1514AD

Solution page 136

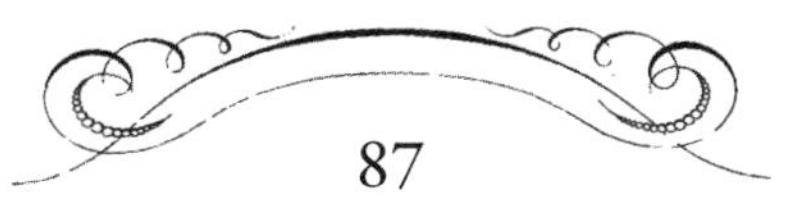

87

AN ODD GIFT

This medieval Spanish riddle poses an interesting intellectual challenge.

It is yours. You create it. You give it to another, who treasures it and holds it close. You keep it still, as you value yourself.

What is it?

Spain
1525AD

Solution page 137

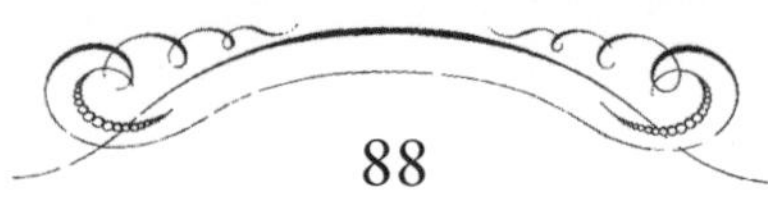

Clock Striking Problem

German mathematician Christoff Rudolff of Augsburg was the first European to draw attention to the Chinese use of decimal notation in maths, in 1530AD, and he also coined the use of the square root symbol, possibly as a stylised 'r' from the Latin word for a square root, 'radix'. He was also the first person to pose the Clock Striking Problem: How many times does a clock's chime strike between noon and midnight? You may assume that the clock strikes only the hour, that it is 12-hour rather than 24-hour, and that the times are inclusive.

Germany
1526AD

Solution page 137

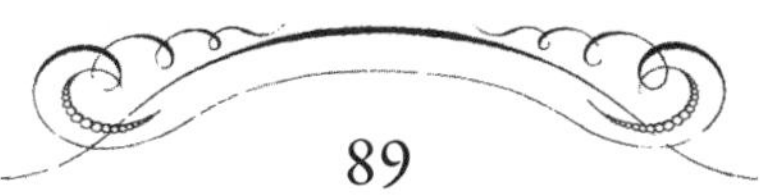

THE DINNER PARTY

This is a puzzle from 16th century Germany, and provides an interesting example of linear indeterminacy, harking back to an 5th century Hindu problem.

A group of 41 people – men, women and children – have been dining at an inn. Their bill comes to 40 groschen, and they divide this up so that each man is paying 3 groschen, each woman is paying 2 groschen, and each child is paying ⅓ groschen.

How many men, women and children made up the group of 41?

GERMANY
1540AD

SOLUTION PAGE 138

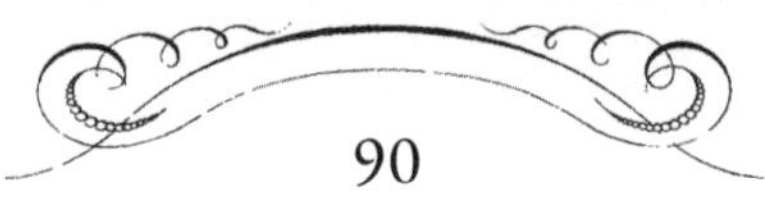

Tricking the Landlord

This is an interesting variant of the Josephus problem that surfaced in medieval Austria, and gained enough popularity to spread through Europe.

It is said that an inn landlord hosts a dinner for 21 friends and family. Being all reasonably well to do, they agree that one member of the group will pay the whole bill for the evening. That person is to be decided by fortune. When the time comes to leave, the landlord's barman will start somewhere in the group and then start counting them in a clockwise direction, with every seventh person counted free to leave the table. When there is but one left, he will pay for the evening.

The barman, however, holds something of a grudge against his master. He decides to make sure that it is his boss who ends up footing the bill. Where does he need to start his count?

Austria
1550AD

Solution page 138

Round and Round

The Sun King, Louis XIV, is remembered as the ruler who oversaw the heights of the French monarchy's trend towards luxury and self-indulgence. His father, Louis XIII, was the king whom the Cardinal de Richlieu served as prime minister, at the time of the setting of Dumas' *The Three Musketeers*. This riddle dates from that period, although admittedly it is slightly more modest in nature than some of the excesses of the time.

What goes around the house and into the house without ever touching the house?

France
1600AD

Solution page 138

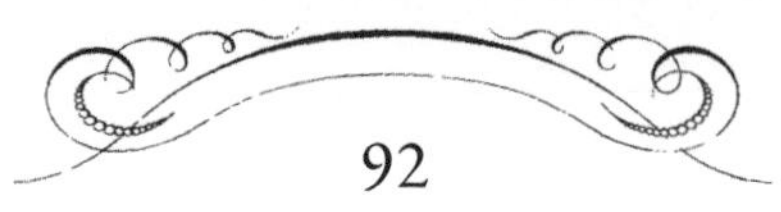

Bachet's Scales

French mathematician Claude Bachet is probably best known for his translation of the book *Arithmetic* by the Greek scholar Diophantus, partly because it was a marginal note in a copy of this volume that revealed the world-famous mathematical problem of Fermat's Last Theorem. But Bachet's work was important in its own right too, and he made important contributions in number theory and other areas.

In 1612, at the age of 31, Bachet produced a book of mathematical puzzles and curiosities, *Problemes Plaisants*. He re-issued it in 1624, in a revised and expanded form. In the larger *Problemes*, he posed this interesting challenge:

If you have a pair of scales, what is the smallest number of weights required to measure the weight of any other object that has an integral weight of between 1 and 40?

France
1624AD

Solution page 139

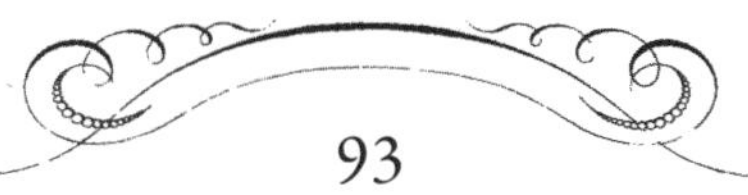

RUPERT'S CUBE

Prince Rupert, Duke of Bavaria was the younger son of a Bavarian noble house in the 17th century. He was at various times a soldier, a pirate, an artist, an inventor and a businessman, rising to considerable levels of achievement in several of those areas. He eventually financed the creation of the Hudson Bay Company, and was its first director.

Imagine a cube with a hole cut through it that leaves the cube in one single piece. Do you imagine that the largest cube able to pass through such a hole would be larger, the same size or smaller than the cube with the hole cut into it?

BAVARIA
1670AD

SOLUTION PAGE 139

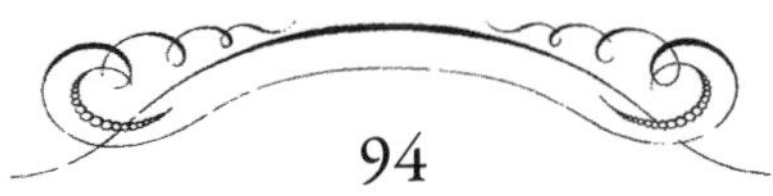

94

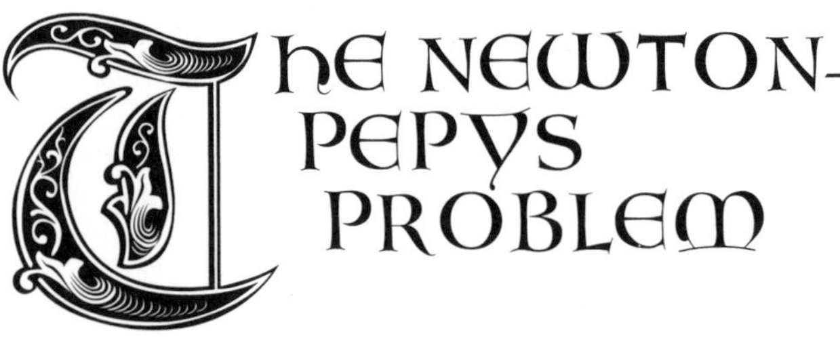

The Newton-Pepys Problem

In 1693, famous English public servant and diarist Samuel Pepys entered into correspondence with Isaac Newton, the father of physics. The topic under discussion related to a wager that Pepys was considering. Pepys wanted to know which of three dice rolls had the greatest odds of success. These were to roll six dice and get at least one 6, to roll twelve dice and get at least two 6s, and to roll eighteen dice and get at least three 6s.

Which is more likely?

England
1693AD

Solution page 140

95

SUNDAY

This riddle was popular in Germany at the end of the 17th century.

There were five men travelling to the church one Sunday. The heavens opened, and it started to rain. The four men who went for cover all got wet. The one man who did not move remained dry. How?

GERMANY
1700AD

SOLUTION PAGE 140

The Tourist

This is one of the more enigmatic of the traditional riddles. It may take some ingenuity to crack.

> I journeyed to the city.
> I stopped there.
> I never went there.
> I came back again.

Switzerland
1700AD

Solution page 141

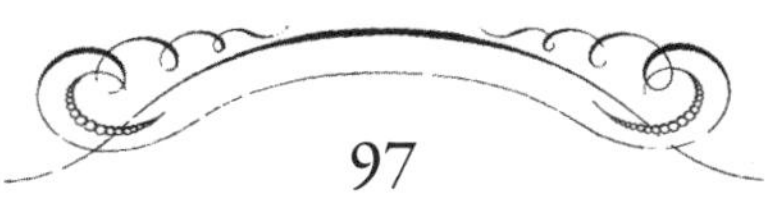

The Bridges of Konigsberg

Königsberg was founded in 1255AD by crusader knights as a base of operations, and swiftly grew in importance to become the capital of East Prussia, finally being incorporated into the German Empire in 1871. It was taken over by the USSR in 1945, and is now the Russian city of Kaliningrad.

The Prussian city of Königsberg straddled the river Pregel, and there were two large, built-up islands in the river connected to each other and the two banks by a set of bridges. It became a matter of near-legendary dispute amongst locals (and visitors) as to whether it was possible to walk through the city crossing each bridge, as shown below, once and only once.

The Swiss mathematician Leonhard Euler finally proved in 1736 that it was impossible. What was his reasoning?

As an aside, it may be interesting to know that one of the bridges was rebuilt in 1935, two were destroyed in World War II and not rebuilt, and two more were replaced with a linked piece of highway after the war. So there are now five bridges, only two of which are antique. A Euler walk is now possible though, albeit one that begins on one island and ends on the other.

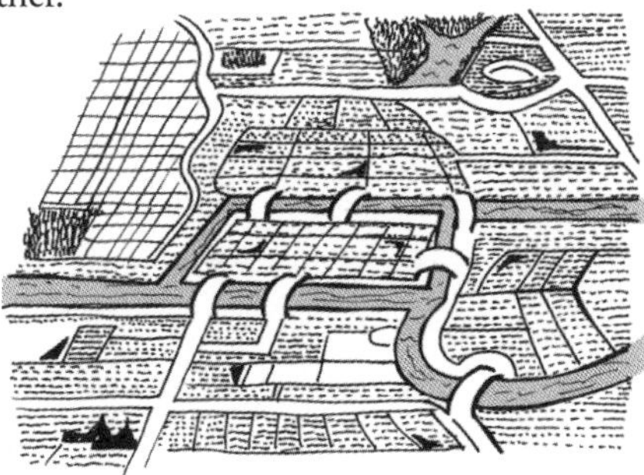

Prussia
1736AD

Solution page 141

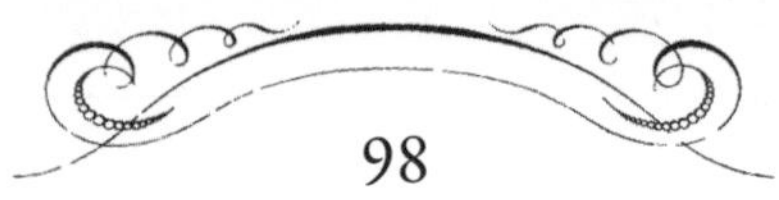

Walking the Walk

Starting from point A in the graph below, it is possible to travel along every line in the graph exactly once. Can you find such a route? This puzzle follows on from Euler's work with the Bridges of Königsberg (see previous page) to pose a rather tangled problem.

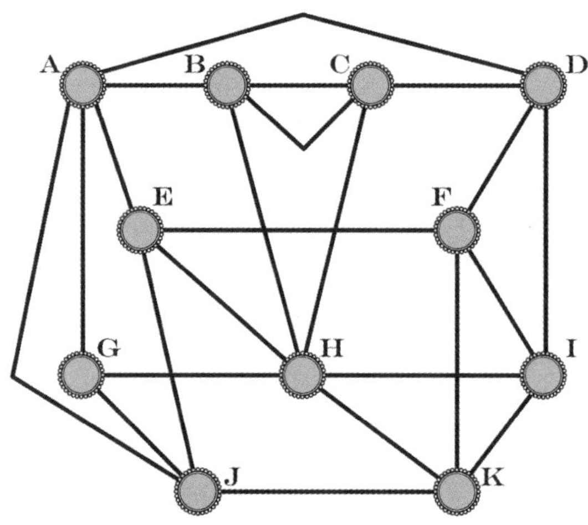

Switzerland
1736AD

Solution page 142

The Tethered Goat

This problem first surfaced in the pages of a society digest, presumably as a practical query from a livestock owner.

Imagine you have a circular field. You want to tie the goat to the fence surrounding the field, and leave it enough slack so that it can graze half of the area of the field. Should the tether be equal to the radius of the field, shorter than the radius, or longer than the radius?

United Kingdom
1748AD

Solution page 142

100

Buffon's Needle

A truly astounding method for approximating pi was discovered by Georges-Louis Leclerc, Comte de Buffon, an 18th century French mathematician and naturalist. The technique derived from a question that Buffon posed in one of his books: if a floor is made up of parallel, equal-width strips of wood, what is the probability that a needle, dropped onto the floor, will cross one of the seams?

The solution to the problem turns out to be reasonably straightforward, albeit a bit tricky to get to. The probability P that the needle will cross a seam depends on the needle's length, L, and the distance between seams, d. Given these, the answer turns out to be $P = {}^{2L}/_{pi*d}$. You can simplify this by making sure that the needle is the same length as the space between seams, in which case $P = {}^{2}/_{pi}$, and therefore $pi = {}^{2}/_{P}$, which broken down, means pi = 2 * (the number of total throws) / (the number of throws where the needle crosses a seam). In other words, amazingly, you can work out pi just by tossing a lot of needles onto a floor and counting how many cross seams.

But why?

France
1777AD

Solution page 143

The Thunderer

This traditional riddle is thought to have originated on the American frontier in the late 18th century.

> I have a cock who needs no grain,
> I keep him as a wonder.
> Every time my cock does crow,
> It lightens, hails and thunders.

United States of America
1800AD

Solution page 143

The Ishango Bone

The second side (B) represents the importance of 10 as a number, by omission. 9 and 11, at either end, bracket 10; and 19 and 21, in the centre, bracket 20. Remember that 10 and 20 are very natural human numbers of importance, given our digits. The third side (C) is the most stunning. It gives 11, 13, 17 and 19 – the prime numbers between 10 and 20, in order. The remaining 7 and 5 on the first side extend the sequence of primes to include all the prime numbers below 20 occurring after 4... the first non-prime number.

Holy Days

The two numbers which give a rectangle the same perimeter length and area are 16 and 18. If perimeter = area, then $2(x+y) = x*y$. This is equivalent to $x = 2 + {}^{4}/_{(y-2)}$. For this equation to work, y-2 has to divide into 4 evenly. In other words, y-2 is 1, 2 or 4; and y is 3, 4 or 6, giving respective values of x of 6, 4 and 3. So 6*3 = 6+6+3+3 = 18, and 4*4 = 4+4+4+4 = 16. The fact that tabooed 17 falls between these numbers made them all the more magical.

FRUSTRUM

Basically, you either know this or you don't, and it turns out the Egyptians did. If h is the height, x is the length of the base and y is the length of the top, then the volume of a truncated pyramid is $h/3*(x^2 + xy + y^2)$. In this case, that's (4*4 + 4*2 + 2*2) * 2, or 56. You can get a rough approximation by taking the average of the upper and lower area and multiplying that by the height – that would give you ((16+4)/2) *6, or 60.

TRIANGLES OF BABYLON

You can either calculate the area of the two triangles, and subtract the larger from the smaller, or work out the area of the trapezoids (height*average length), and multiply that by 3. The latter option is complicated by lack of immediate easy data – we don't know precisely how high the trapezoid is, nor how long the top and bottom lines are. The area of an equilateral triangle of side-length s is $s^{2 * (\text{root } 3)}/4$. So for the larger triangle, it's 25/4 * root 3, and for the smaller, it's 9/4 * root 3. That's approximately 10.8 - 3.9, or 6.9 square units.

Ahmes' Loaves

Ancient Egyptian techniques of division were unwieldy, and you're not expected to be able to guess how they did it. For this puzzle, the trick lies in thinking about the five men getting identical pieces. First off, divide one loaf into 5. That takes care of $^1/_5$. Divide the remaining two loaves into thirds; that gives you five lots of $^1/_3$, with an extra $^1/_3$. Cut the remaining $^1/_3$ into five pieces, giving you $^1/_{15}$s. Then each man gets $^1/_3$ + $^1/_5$ + $^1/_{15}$, and Ahmes would have understood exactly what you meant. Note there are infinite other possible answers here, all equivalent and fitting the question – that was one of the flaws of ancient Egyptian fractional technique. To give just one example, you could cut the loaves into 5, 6 and 11, cutting the remaining 6ths and 11ths into 5 in turn, to give $^1/_5$ + $^1/_6$ + $^1/_{11}$ + $^1/_{30}$ + $^1/_{55}$. Nevertheless, $^1/_3$ + $^1/_5$ + $^1/_{15}$ is the most simple solution.

As I Was Going to Amenemhet III's

Nothing too complicated here, just fiddly. Multiplying by 7 each time, we get: 7 houses, 49 cats, 343 mice, 2,401 sheaves of wheat, and 16,807 hekats of grain. Together, that comes to 19,607.

A QUESTION OF QUANTITY

Ahmes deals with this problem through *Regula Falsi.* In order to remove the quarter, he starts by assuming that the missing quantity, x, is 4. Then 4 + (4 * 1 / 4) = 5, which is a third of the required sum of fifteen. That means his first guess is three times too small, and x must be 12.

A FRACTIONAL ISSUE

In terms of modern mathematics, this question is asking you to find $^2/_3 + {}^1/_{15} + {}^1/_x = 1$. We know now that $^2/_3$ is equivalent to $^{10}/_{15}$, and 1 to $^{15}/_{15}$, so the answer of $^4/_{15}$ is simple. The Egyptians took a different route. First, they multiplied through by the lowest common denominator, 15, to get 10 + 1 + y = 15, and so y was obviously 4. y is 15*x, so x=$^1/_{15}$*y, or 4*$^1/_{15}$. That meant doubling $^1/_{15}$ twice, using Ahmes' table. We don't have that, but we can think in multiple fractions instead. Reducing $^4/_{15}$ down, the largest unit fraction that we can remove and that leaves a unit fraction behind is $^1/_5$, leaving $^1/_{15}$, so the answer is $^1/_5 + {}^1/_{15}$.

STRONG GRAIN

From our point of view, pesu 10 barley is worth 4.5* pesu 45 barley (from $^{45}/_{10}$), so a fair sum would be 450 hekats. Ahmes gets there by first pointing out that 45 is 35 greater than 10. He then divides that 35 by the 10, to get a unit value of 3 + ½. Then he multiplies this by the 100 hekats for 350 hekats, as the value of the difference, and then adds it back to the original 100 hekats for the total value, getting 450 hekats.

PROGRESSIVE LOAVES

First of all, you need to work out a standard decrement, or gap, that gives the correct ratio of $^{1}/_{7}$ of the top 3 shares = the bottom 2. You know 5, 4, 3, 2, 1 is wrong, but try it, and you'll find that 3 (from 2+1) - 1 $^{5}/_{7}$ ($^{12}/_{7}$) = 1 $^{2}/_{7}$. Try again with a gap of 2, and you have 9, 7, 5, 3, 1. Now the difference in ratio is 4 - (21 * $^{1}/_{7}$), or 1. The ratio is narrowing, by $^{1}/_{7}$ for every half-point of gap between numbers. We need to get to 0, which means a further three and a half points of gap on from 2 – the first gap to fill the answer is 5 ½. Calculating up from 1, that gives us 1, 6.5, 12, 17.5 and 23, which total to 60. We need them to total to 100, which means multiplying everything by $^{100}/_{60}$, or 1 ⅔. So our final results are 1 ⅔, 10 $^{4}/_{6}$, 20, 29 $^{1}/_{6}$ and 38 ⅓, and the difference between shares is 9 + $^{1}/_{6}$.

DATES

Try to answer this problem by reducing the question to fractions and then working it through in the Egyptian style, with only unit fractions, and you'll find it rapidly becomes tryingly complex – particularly without an Egyptian fraction-doubling table to hand. *Regula Falsi* provides a much better approach. Let's try 3, to even out the initial thirds. 3 + 2 is 5, and ⅓ of that is 1 ⅔, leaving 3 ⅓. That's a third of 10, the value we want, so multiple our initial guess by 3, to get 9. 9+6 = 15, and ⅔ of that is 10.

THE RULE OF THREE

Simply stated, the Rule of Three is that if we have an equation where a/b = c/x, then by multiplying out, a*x = b*c, and therefore x=b*c/a. Ahmes answers the problem by saying that if the heap was 7 (for easy calculation), then 7 + (7/7) would be 19. It isn't, it's 8. That means 7 is as far short of the answer as 8 is of 19. So multiplying 7 by the amount required to turn 8 into 19 (which has to be 19/8) gives the correct answer – and it does, 16.625 (that .625 is ⅝). Give yourself a bonus point if you broke this down into an Ahmes-friendly 16 + ½+ ⅛. If you're wondering where the Golden Rule comes in, consider the question as 8/7ths of x = 19, or 8x/7=19/1, so 8/7 = 19/x. By the Golden Rule, that then means x = 7 * 19/8.

PROGRESSIVE SHARES

Ahmes reasons that the portions must average to 1 (10 hekats / 10 people), and there are only 9 differences between the ten shares. To find where he has to start his sequences (descending), he calculates half of the desired difference, $^1/_{16}$, and multiplies that by the 9, to give ½ + $^1/_{16}$. Adding this to the average value gives him the largest of the terms, 1 + ½ + $^1/_{16}$. It is fascinating to realize that this is an exact practical rendering of modern formulae for discovering the largest term of an arithmetic sequence. The smallest, in case you are interested, turns out to be ¼ + ⅛ + $^1/_{16}$ of a hekat.

SQUARING THE CIRCLE

The title, here, is the hint. Draw a square of 9*9 that exactly fits the circle, and then divide that square into a three-by-three grid of 9 chunks, each with an area of 9 units sq. You'd get greater accuracy if you divided it into fifths or sevenths than into thirds, but trisecting will do. Look at the grid over the circle, and you'll see that roughly speaking, the circle cuts the corner squares in half, and leaves the other squares intact. If you actually cut the corners in half, producing an octagon, it does follow the circle quite closely. Add up the number of chunks in your octagon, and it comes to 7 pieces of 9 units sq, or 63 units sq. Ahmes fudges the assumption that 63 is almost 64, which is a convenient 8*8, and says that a circle of diameter 9 is equal in area to a square of width 8, and gives the answer as 64*6 = 384. The more obvious answer, from the octagon, is 63*6 = 378, which is what you should have. The modern answer, by the way, is 381.7 – so either way, we're not far out.

SQUARE TRIAL

We know that $x^2 + y^2 = 100$. If y = x*3/4, then 3x=4y. The simplest Regula Falsi we can try for the second equation is that x is 4 and y is 3. Putting that into the first equation, we get 16 + 9 = 25, rather than 100. We are 4 times out, but we can't just multiply x and y by 4, as we're looking at squares. We have to take the square root of 4 to give 2, and multiply by that, so x is 8 and y is 6. Note that the original author, perhaps concerned about cases where the factor isn't a neat square number, instead took the square roots of 25 and 100 (5 and 10 respectively), and observed that they were out by a factor of 2, and derived the 2 that way.

SUMERIAN RIDDLE

The riddle refers to a school.

RAMESSES' STAR

The knack to this puzzle is continually circling around the star in the same direction, always selecting your previous starting point as your next end point. For example, let's imagine the star's circles are lettered from A to J, starting at the top point and working clockwise around the perimeter line. Then one sequence of moves which will fill 9 spots is as follows: Start at A and jump to D (A>D), then H>A, E>H, B>E, J>B, F>I, C>F, J>C and G>J.

THE RIDDLE OF THE SPHINX

The answer is man, who crawls when newborn, walks upright when adult, and requires a cane in old age. Oedipus was the one who finally got the riddle right, leading the Sphinx to hurl herself to her death from her lofty perch.

THE QUIET ONE

It is a river.

VISITORS

The stars.

CRETANS

There are several possible approaches. First of all, Epimenides might simply be wrong, in which case there is no paradox. Alternatively, if some Cretans are liars, that can include Epimenides, but not, say, his mother, so he's lying without causing paradox. Or the statement of the paradox itself may itself be a lie; he may have said no such thing. Taking a common sense approach, you can argue that the statement doesn't have to be an absolute and immutable declaration – no-one lies all the time – and thus again, there is no paradox.

ZENO'S DICHOTOMY

Zeno is assuming that there are an infinite number of subdivisions of space, but only a finite number of subdivisions of time. Both of these are arbitrary assumptions. Modern molecular physics suggests that space does have a minimum subdivision at the subatomic level, but even discounting that, if space can be infinitely divisible, why not time as well? Then the two infinities cancel out – there may be infinite half-way stages, but it's OK, because you have infinite moments to get to them.

Zenos' Arrow

On one level, it's clear that objects do move, and possess a quality of momentum. But that's not the answer. Interestingly, if you look at reality at the quantum level, it becomes clear that Zeno was absolutely right. If reality is viewed as a purely spatial construct, mediated through a series of time-slices – the classical view of the real world – then there would indeed be no logical point for motion to occur in. Quantum mechanics has shown conclusively that at the subatomic level, if you know an object's position, you cannot know its momentum, and vice versa. In other words, position and momentum are incompatible. If you can say Zeno's Arrow is exactly at point X, then you cannot say it is moving, and vice-versa. It never occurred to Zeno that space and time might be tied together so intimately to form our reality, but his intuition was spot on. If that's not bad enough, consider the Quantum Zeno effect, so named in 1977 – if you watch a Quantum system continuously, its normal passage through time is interrupted. In effect, watching Zeno's arrow that closely actually does make it stand still.

Zeno's Stadium

At first glance, Zeno is making the stupid mistake of confusing relative speed with absolute speed. A passes B quickly because B is also in motion. It should be utter rubbish – except that modern physics suggests that if two spaceships approach each other from opposite directions, both travelling at the speed of light, each will appear to the other to be travelling at the speed of light, not twice the speed of light. Looks like Zeno might have a point here after all...

ACHILLES AND THE TORTOISE

As with the Dichotomy, Zeno is discounting the cases where space and time are both equally divisible or indivisible. In either case, it becomes possible for Achilles to meet the Tortoise at exactly the same spot in space–time, and then to pass it. Also, Quantum uncertainty at these super-miniscule distances makes it impossible to talk meaningfully about moving a certain tiny space in a certain tiny time – it can be one or other, but not both.

THE HEAP

If you want to retain the notion of the word 'heap' having any meaning, then there has to be an arbitrary point at which the heap stops being a heap, and earns itself some more diminutive adjective. The fact that the word 'heap' doesn't tell us precisely when that occurs is a fault of the vagueness of language, rather than any logical inconsistency. The only alternative positions are that no collection of grains is ever a heap – rather futile, as you can then derive the almost total meaninglessness of language from such a standpoint – or that a single grain can in fact be a heap, which is only a little less unhelpful.

Four Brothers

The brothers are the four classical elements – water, that runs and runs; fire, that devours; earth, that soaks up moisture; and air, with its howling and whistling.

The Shoot

The answer is a mountain.

The Nursery

The riddle refers to a watermelon, with its green skin, white pith, red flesh and seeds.

The Luo River Scroll

The Lo Shu is the first magic square, where all straight lines and corner diagonals add up to 15, and opposing pairs of numbers add up to 10. It is the only 3x3 magic square possible.

Buridan's Ass

The 17th century Dutch philosopher Spinoza suggested that in fact there was nothing paradoxical about the principle. Unpleasant as it may be, some dilemmas are so convoluted as to lead the victim down a third path of disastrous inactivity, even to the point of death sometimes.

Hui Shi's Third Paradox

This is an issue of relativity, in keeping with Hui Shi's philosophical beliefs. From a viewpoint on a massive scale, the differences between mountain and marsh – or even heaven and earth – are so miniscule as to be non-existent. The obverse, that from a microscopic viewpoint all worldly things are vast, also ties in to some of his other paradoxes. The point is valid; any differentiation only has meaning within a set scale, and so from a certain point of view, any perceived difference is meaningless.

The Ladder of Horus

Euclid's formula provides a method of generating Pythagorean triples. If you take two integers, m and n, so that exactly one of them is odd and the two share no common divisors, then the following equations will generate the Pythagorean triples: $x=2mn$, $y=m^2-n^2$, and $z=m^2+n^2$. There are 3 triples with a z of less than 20: 3-4-5, 5-12-13 and 8-15-17.

THE ZERO PROOF

The flaw in the proof lies in assuming that you can apply the associative law to an infinitely long calculation. Generally, this isn't true. The associative law assumes you have a certain number of terms. Infinity has an uncertain number, so you can't just rearrange the sums. Or look at it this way. Infinity is uncountable, so in both cases, you have infinite pairs of zero terms stretching off. You can either start that chain with a 1 or not, but that doesn't alter the fact that it's the chains themselves that are equal, not the whole expression.

CROCODILE TEARS

If the mother says that she will get the baby back, the crocodile is free to eat him and prove her wrong. If she says that the crocodile will eat the baby, and the crocodile does, then it must give the baby back – but if it acknowledges this and gives the baby back, the mother is no longer right, and so the crocodile does not have to give him back after all. This is irreconcilable, and the crocodile may well decide that since both options are impossible, it is free to do as it wishes, and eat the baby – or to gruesomely split the difference. Some thinkers have suggested that the best course is to turn the statement back on the crocodile – so the mother responds, "I predict that if I correctly predict the fate of the my baby, then you will return him. Otherwise, you will eat him." This would unarguably cancel out the crocodile's options, providing that it is taken to count as a valid prediction.

THE SIEVE OF ERATOSTHENES

The sieve's simplicity is breathtakingly elegant. To find all the prime numbers in a range, write them all out starting from 1, and then starting from 2, go through and cross off all the multiples of each uncrossed number. (1 is not generally considered prime). So you do not cross off 2, but cross off 4, 6, 8, 10, 12, etc. 3 is uncrossed, so it is prime, but you cross off 6, 9, 12, 15, etc. 4 is crossed, ignore it, but 5 is uncrossed and prime, and you cross off 10, 15, 20, etc. Go on through to the square root of the number, because any larger divisor must be paired to a smaller divisor. 100 is 25*4, but you'll have hit that possibility at 4 already. 10*10 represents the largest possible smaller divisor. The sieve is so-named because if you write it out as a grid, the primes are the holes.

Incidentally, the original proof that there is an infinity of primes is as follows: assume that the list of numbers p1, p2, p3 ... p# is the full list of prime numbers. If you multiply all of them together, and then add 1 to the total, you get a new number, P. It is mathematical fact that every non-prime number is a multiple of one or more prime numbers, because only primes are indivisible. So either P is a prime number itself, which makes it a new prime to add to the list, or it is divisible by a prime number that is not already on the list. P cannot be divisible by a prime on the list already, because you got it by multiplying them all together and then adding 1. This would mean that your prime on the list would have to be smaller than 1, which is not allowed. So, in other words, either P is prime, or it is divisible by a prime you don't already know – and there are therefore always more primes.

Archimedes' Revenge

This puzzle describes a complex indeterminate polynomial equation that must have an integer solution. The sheer vastness of the numbers concerned makes it extremely difficult. The answer turns out to be 7.76×10^{206544} – a truly gargantuan amount. Number theorists have suggested that if you took a sphere with a diameter equal to the width of our galaxy, and shrunk each of the cattle to the size of an electron, they still wouldn't fit.

The generally accepted text of Archimedes' Revenge has a certain poetic beauty. It goes like this... If thou art diligent and wise, O stranger, compute the number of cattle of the Sun, who once upon a time grazed on the fields of the Thrinacian isle of Sicily, divided into four herds of different colours, one milk white, another a glossy black, a third yellow and the last dappled. In each herd were bulls, mighty in number according to these proportions: Understand, stranger, that the white bulls were equal to a half and a third of the black bulls together with the whole of the yellow bulls, while the black were equal to the fourth part of the dappled and a fifth, together with, once more, the whole of the yellow. Observe further that the remaining bulls, the dappled, were equal to a sixth part of the white and a seventh, together with all of the yellow.

These were the proportions of the cows: The white were precisely equal to the third part and a fourth of the whole herd of the black; while the black were equal to the fourth part once more of the dappled and with it a fifth part, when all, including the bulls, went to pasture together. Now the dappled in four parts were equal in number to a fifth part and a sixth of the yellow herd. Finally the yellow were in number equal to a sixth part and a seventh of the white herd. If thou canst accurately tell, O stranger, the number of cattle of the Sun, giving separately the number of well-fed bulls and again the number of females according to each colour, thou wouldst not be called unskilled or ignorant of numbers, but not yet shalt thou be numbered among the wise.

But come, understand also all these conditions regarding the cattle of the Sun. When the white bulls mingled their number with the black, they stood firm, equal in depth and breadth, and the plains of Thrinacia, stretching far in all ways, were filled with their multitude. Again, when the yellow and the dappled bulls were gathered into one herd they stood in such a manner that their number, beginning from one, grew slowly greater till it completed a triangular figure, there being no bulls of other colours in their midst nor none of them lacking. If thou art able, O stranger, to find out all these things and gather them together in your mind, giving all the relations, thou shalt depart crowned with glory and knowing that thou hast been adjudged perfect in this species of wisdom.

THE NINE CHAPTERS

The book presents a fairly sophisticated matrix solution process to answer the puzzle, but it is simpler for us to solve it by algebra. We have three conditions for making one measure, which we can represent as three equations, $2a + b = 1$, $3b + c = 1$ and $4c + a = 1$. This can be solved by substitution. For example, multiply the last equation by 2 to give $8c + 2a = 2$, and subtract this from the first equation, so $2a + b - 8c - 2a = 1 - 2$, or $b - 8c = -1$. This means that $b = 8c - 1$, and we can substitute b in the second equation to get $3(8c-1) + c = 1$, or $25c - 3 = 1$. That gives us $25c = 4$, or $c = 4/25$ths of a measure. Similarly, $b = 7/25$ths and $a = 9/25$ths.

The Cistern Problem

The first tap provides 48 in 12 hours, or 4/hour. The second tap is twice as fast, so provides 8/hour. The third tap removes 6/hour. The net balance is 6 per hour, so the cistern will fill in 8 hours.

Dog and Hare

We know that a chase of 125pu closes a gap of 50pu. This means that the gap closes 1pu for each 2.5pu chased. So a 30pu gap requires 30*2.5pu to close, or 75pu.

The Chickens

Simple algebra will let you solve this puzzle once you've reduced it to appropriate equations. Assuming that the number of purchasers is x, and the actual price is p. Then we know that 9x = p+11, and 6x = p-16. Subtract the latter equation from the former, and 9x - 6x = p + 11 - (p-16), or 3x = 27. So x=9. Then p = 9x - 11, which is 81 - 11, or 70. There are 9 purchasers, paying 70 wen between them.

Leg and Thigh

Look at the square inside the triangle, and you'll see that the two smaller triangles it creates are miniature versions of the larger triangle. They share the same angles, and are therefore equivalent, just different sizes. If x is the square's side length, then the sides of one of the smaller triangles on the ku will be ku-x and x in length, not counting the hypotenuse. Because the triangles are equivalent, the ratio of length between the sides must stay the same as in the larger triangle. So ku:kou = (ku-x):x, and x=ku*kou/(ku+kou), or in this case, 60/17 ch'ih.

Men Buy a Horse

The trick here is to represents the men's statements in algebraic form, and then you'll have three simultaneous equations with three unknowns, which is solvable. Noting that they all have whole numbers, the first man has 16 yuan, the second man has 10 yuan, and the third man has 6 yuan.

They're footsteps.

Posthumous Twins

The usual answer to this problem is to take the common claimant, the mother, and compare the two children's shares to her share. The ratio of son:mother and mother:daughter is 2:1. The son therefore gets twice as much as the mother, who gets twice as much as the daughter. So the shares are 4/7 to the son, 2/7 to the mother, and 1/7 to the daughter.

The Ship of Theseus

This is really a philosophical question rather than a simple paradox. Aristotle maintained that it is the form of something that defines its reality, and that the materials used, its content, are of lesser import. In that sense, it is definitely the same ship. Japanese culture assumes this principle as a general fact. In an absolutely rigorous definition of the "same" ship, then no, once one piece is removed, its integrity is violated. Some orthodox Jewish taboos seem to follow this latter view. A utilitarian view might suggest that the ship's final form would have been settled the moment Theseus left it for the last time, and so the first Athenian repair would have invalidated it. In the end though, these are all opinions, and the choice is yours.

MEN FIND A PURSE

The lowest sums are 23 in the purse, 9 for the first man, 16 for the second man, and 13 for the third man. Fibonacci finds the answer as follows: "consider the second man. His cash, y, is ½ that of the first man's cash, x, plus the purse's cash, p. The third man's cash, z, is ⅓ (y +p). The first man's is ¼ (z +p). Multiply the fractions of x, y and z, to get a common denominator 1/24, and subtract the 1 from the 24 to find the total in the purse, 23. Then to find the total value, he adds 1 to the bottom of each fraction, to give ⅓, ¼ and 1/5, and multiplies through again, for 1/60. This time he adds the terms together, to find the total value, 61. He then takes those second fractions, and splits them into pairs, one for each man. He subtracts 1 one from the first of each the pair, multiplies both terms together, and adds them to give each man's share. So ⅓ and ¼ become ½ * ¼, or ⅛, and 1 + 8 is 9 for the first share. ¼ and 1/5 give 1/15, or a share of 16, and 1/5 and ⅓ give 1/12, or 13". Award yourself a lot of extra points if you used this inductive method rather than something more... sensible.

THE UNWANTED

The answer is counterfeit money.

THE FIVE SONS

The trick to this puzzle is to convert the requirements into simultaneous equations, and see how many ways it can be solved. For each son, the total number of each type of cask added together will be 9, and when you multiply those numbers by the amount of wine each can hold, they will sum to 18. It turns out that there are eight possible solutions that give 9 casks and 18 pints. You then need five different solutions from that eight that can be added together to give just 9 of each type of cask. This can be done in three different ways. Labelling the types of cask v-z from 4pt to empty for brevity's sake, one brother will always get 3v+w+x+y+3z. The other four will get any two pairs of: (v+3w+2x+y+2z and 2v+w+2x+3y+z), (v+3w+x+3y+z and 2v+w+3x+y+2z), and (v+2w+3x+2y+z and 2v+2w+x+2y+2z)

SUN TZU'S CLASSIC PROBLEM

The answer is 23. In general, for each divisor x, you have to find a multiple of the other divisors that is one more than a multiple of x. Call this new multiple a. You then multiply a by the remainder you got after dividing by x, and add this sum to the equivalent figures from the other remainders. If the total is more than your divisors multiplied together, subtract that value and check again. The number remaining is the answer. That produces a unique result for any number of divisors, so long as they are co-prime. So in this puzzle, *3 leaves 2, *5 leaves 3 and *7 leaves 2. The first multiple of 5 * 7 that is 1 greater than a multiple of 3 is 70. Similarly, for *5, it's 21, and for x6, it's 15. (2 * 70) + (3 * 21) + (2 * 15) = 233. Subtract (3 * 5 * 7), or 105, to get 128. Subtract it again to get 23.

THE TROUBLE WITH CAMELS

To solve this puzzle, you really need to notice that ½ + ⅓ + 1/9 is 17/18ths. The lawyer lends a camel to the herd, bringing it to 18 beasts. Then the eldest son gets ½, or 9 camels; the middle son gets ⅓, or 6 camels, and the luckless younger son gets 1/9, or 2 camels. 9 + 6 + 2 is 17, so the lawyer's camel is still available for him to reclaim.

THE SNAIL AND THE WELL

No, the snail will never climb out. The amount it climbs depreciates by 10% a day, so on day two it climbs 1.8 feet, then 1.62, 1.46, 1.31, 1.18, 1.06 and finally, on day eight, 0.95 feet. It loses a foot each night, so if it hasn't made it out by the end of day eight, it may as well give up and enjoy the well. Its maximum height, which falls on day seven, will be the net result of each previous day's climbs (1 + 0.8 + 0.62 + 0.46 + 0.31 + 0.18) + that day's pre-slip climb, 1.06 – a total of 4.43 feet. Close, but not quite close enough.

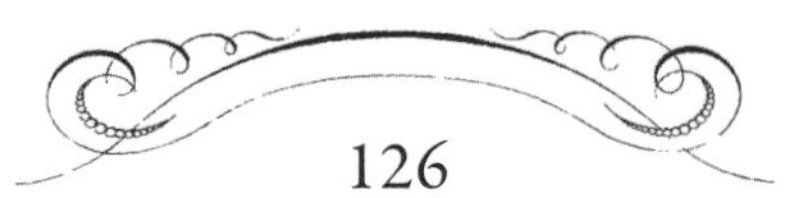

Alcuin's Camel

Alcuin's solution is confused, but a proper solution is as follows. If it tries to do the whole first load in one trip, it will arrive with no grain left, unable to get back to the origin. So it must do it in stages. Coming and going is inefficient, because of the camel's feed requirement, so the stages are placed so as to minimise the distance travelled, whilst avoiding abandoning any grain. This puts them at 25% and 50% distance. The first trip, the camel starts with 30 modia of grain and travels to and from the 7.5 league mark, leaving 15 modia there and returning with 0. The second trip, the camel starts with 30 modia again, eats 7.5 to stage 1, replenishes itself back to 30, continues on to stage 2, drops off 7.5 modia, and then uses the remaining 15 going back to the origin. In the final stage, the camel takes the last 30, replenishes the 7.5 it has eaten at stage 1, leaving nothing, and does the same at stage 2. Finally, it travels the last 15 leagues, eating 15 modia, and arriving with 15 modia.

Brothers and Sisters

Alcuin's solution is optimal. "First of all, my sister and I got into the boat and crossed. Having crossed the river, I let my sister out and recrossed the river. Then the sisters of the two men who remained on the bank got in. When these women had gotten out of the boat, my sister, who had already gone across, got in and brought the boat back to us. She then got out, and the two brothers crossed in the boat. Then, one of the brothers and his sister crossed over to us. However, I and the brother who piloted the boat went across while my sister remained behind. When we had been taken to the [other] side, one of the other women took the boat back across, and my sister came across to us with her at the same time. Then the man whose sister had remained on the other side got in the boat and brought it back with her. Thus the crossing was accomplished, with no one being defiled." Quite.

ALCUIN'S FLASKS

No, it's not possible in this instance. There are five possible solutions, which you can discover by considering the different ways of distributing the full flasks in terms of the way 10 can factor down to three numbers, none greater than 5. Alcuin divides them up into 10 half-full / 5 full 5 empty / 5 full 5 empty. Two solutions give different distributions – 1f 8h 1e / 4f 2h 4e / 5f 0h 5e and 2f 6h 2e / 3f 4h 3e / 5f 0h 5e, but in both cases, one son ends up with no half-full flasks. The remaining two give each son at least one of each, but two sons get the same distribution – 2f 6h 2e / 4f 2h 4f / 4f 2h 4f and 3f 4h 3e / 3f 4h 3e / 4f 2h 4f. Note that the number of full and empty flasks is always the same; this stays true even if the number of flasks varies, and is the reason why when factoring, we can't go above half the total – 6 full means 6 empty, which is more than the allowed share of flasks.

THE EASTERN MERCHANT

Alcuin's answer is to go as far as he can with the most expensive item, and then juggle the rest to reach 100 animals in total. He says, "If you take 10 nine times and add five, you get 95; that is, 19 camels are bought for 95 solidi. Add to this one solidus for an ass, making 96. Then, take 20 times four, making 80 – that is, 20 sheep for four solidi. Add 19 and one and 80, making 100. This is the number of animals. Then add 95 and one and four, making 100 solidi. Hence there are 100 beasts and 100 solidi." Whilst not a general solution for puzzles of this type, it can at least act as a Regula Falsi basis for a solution.

Alcuin's Grain

To start with, the possible maximum numbers are bounded. 6 men, 1 woman and 2 children use up all the grain, as do 1 man, 8 women and 2 children, and 1 man, 1 woman and 30 children. This gives you upper bounds. 2 men would need 18 others, but then 3 women would leave 16 children, and 4 women would leave just 12, so it's not 2 men. 3 men need 17 others, but 1 woman leaves 18 children, and 2 leave 14. With 4 men, it's even worse – right from the start, there are too few people to reach 20. So it has to be 1 man, and by similar elimination, it turns out to be 5 women and 14 children.

The Hundred Steps

The trick is to notice that taking the top and bottom number together in turn gives a constant value, so that a simple multiplication gives you the answer. In this case, it is simplest to assume there's a zero step as well, and then there are 50 pairs of steps adding up to 100 (100+0, 99+1, etc), down to 51+49. 50 remains as an odd central step. So the answer is 50*100 +50, or 5050.

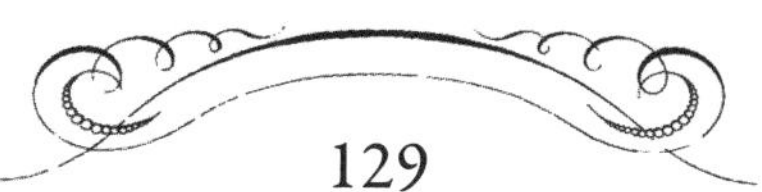

Alcuin's Riddle

The 'beast' is a comb, which was made of ivory. The two heads refer to the carved ends of the comb, which were in the shape of lions' heads.

The Josephus Problem

The most straightforward way to tackle this problem is just to count. The second to last man would have been standing in 16th place.

The Explorer's Problem

From a starting point of zero, speeds of 10mph and 15mph diverge at a rate of $\frac{1}{3}$ of an hour per 10 miles travelled. We need a gap of 2 hours between them, so that's 6*$\frac{1}{3}$hrs, and 6*10 miles or 60 miles. It takes six hours to do that distance at 10mph, and 4 at 15mph, so sunset is 5 hours away, and the required speed is $^{60}/_{5}$ or 12mph.

Monkey Nuts

You can solve this by trial and error, but it is painstaking. A better approach is to convert the four iterations into simultaneous equations with five unknowns: the original total, after the first sailor, after the second sailor, after the third sailor, and in the morning. Reducing these equations down will leave you with a resulting equation in two unknowns, which is much easier to figure out. It helps to realize that each time, the pile that is being hidden must itself be divisible by 3 if the monkey's one coconut is added. The equations you derive can be reduced further, but the answer is that there were 79 coconuts initially.

The Book of Precious Things

There are 2,678 possible answers to the puzzle, of which Abu Kamil found 2,676 in his Book. One possible solution is 39 ducks, 9 doves, 27 ringdoves, 22 larks and 3 hens, but obviously we can't give them all. To solve the number of answers, assemble the birds into indivisible groups that cost as much as the number of birds they contain. There are five -- (a) 1 hen (1 for 1); (b) 1 duck and 2 doves (3 for 3); (c) 2 ducks, 1 dove and 2 larks (5 for 5); (d) 2 ducks and 3 ringdoves (also 5 for 5); and (e) 3 ducks and 4 larks (7 for 7). The challenge then becomes finding how many ways you can combine these groups to hit 100, which is a more manageable question. You need at least one of (a) and (d), and then at least either one or more of (c) or one or more of both (b) and (e). Note (b) + (e) and (c)+(d) both equal 10 birds, and using these groups, any amount of shortfall can be made up with hens.

A Medieval Riddle

It's an onion, but the riddle is interesting for the earthiness that it displays on the part of the church at the time.

The Mariner

The answer is an anchor.

The Memory Wheel

The wheels are used for generating a full sequence of binary tokens. The smaller wheel represents all possible two-digit tokens, ie. the numbers 0–3, but not in sequence; the larger wheel similarly represents three-digit tokens, the numbers 0–7. Starting from one point, read your two (or three) digits clockwise round the wheel. For the next digit, move clockwise one position. So the small wheel is actually code for 0,0; 0,1; 1,1; 1,0. It is possible to construct memory wheels for an arbitrary number of digits; the number of positions in the wheel will be 1 greater than the maximum number the largest token can describe. The Sanskrit YamAtArAjabhAnasalagAm is actually the same device – it is a nonsense word, with long and short syllables representing binary positions. It can be rendered just as easily as 1000101110, where a short 'a' syllable is a 1 and a long 'A' syllable is a 0. It was used to remember the eight poetic forms, or Ganas, of Sanskrit poetry. The two extra digits, in this instance, are there as duplications of the first two, because the word is not laid out in a circle.

JIA XIAN'S TRIANGLE

A little careful examination should make the ancient Chinese system of Rod Numerals fairly obvious. The Triangle itself is easy to figure out if you start from the top: the nodes in each line are the sum of the nodes feeding into it from the line above. We know this as Pascal's Triangle, and it is a surprisingly powerful and intricate tool for being such a simple construction.

THE OLD ONE

The answer is a church bell in a steeple.

THE TROUBLE WITH RABBITS

When we start, we have 1 pair. In the first month, the rabbits give birth to a new pair, for 2 pairs. In the second month, just the first rabbits breed again, producing 3 pairs. In the third month, the first new pair also breeds, so we get two more pairs, for a total of 5. In the fourth month, we have three breeding pairs, for a total of 8 – and so on for 13, 21, 34, 55, 89, 144, 233 and finally 377. The pattern 1, 1, 2, 3, 5, 8, 13, ... should be familiar: it is the Fibonacci Sequence, named for Fibonacci, who set the puzzle in the *Liber Abaci*. It is one the best-known mathematical sequences, and finds expression throughout nature, art and science.

The Ring Game

Through the multiplications, the different elements of the answer – seat number, finger number and joint number – are put into separate digits of the final total. Take away 350, the base value of the first set of multiplications, and the digits of the result give you seat, finger and joint. For example, someone in the 8th seat, with a ring on the 2nd joint of finger 4, will result in a total of 8*2 = 16, +5 = 21, *5 = 105, +10 = 115. (115 + 4) * 10 = 1190, and +2 = 1192. 1192-350 = 842, which breaks back down to 8 - 4 - 2.

The Well

Fibonacci uses *Regula Falsi* to derive the answer to this puzzle. First he points out that from the top of each tower to its base to the well and back up to the tower top is an equilateral triangle. The birds arrive at the same time, so the length of the hypotenuse in both triangles is the same. Assuming that the taller tower is 'A' paces from the well and the shorter is 'Z', then from Pythagoras's Theorem, we know that $A^2 + 40^2 = Z^2 + 30^2$. To solve this, he says, suppose A is 10, making Z 40. Then that side of the equation will be 100 + 1600 (1700), and the other side will be 1600 + 900 (2500). That's an erroneous imbalance of 800. Try again with A=15 and Z=35. Now we get 1825 = 2125, which is an imbalance of 300. We have increased A by 5 and found that we are 500 closer to our answer. We need to be 300 closer still, so increase A by 3. A=18 and Z=32 gives us 1924 on both sides. The well is 18 paces from the taller tower.

Tartaglia's Wine

There isn't any general solution to this problem, but rendering the limits of the jugs as a graph and exploring and moving from boundary node to boundary node can help. Anyhow. The optimal answer is to take the following steps: Fill the 3pt jug, empty it into the 5pt jug, fill the 3pt jug from the 8pt jug again, then fill the 5pt jug from 3pt jug. This gives you 1pt in the 3pt jug, 5pt in the 5, and 2pts in the 8. Empty the 5pt jug into the 8pt and empty the 1pt into the 5pt, giving you 0, 1 and 7pts. Then fill the 3pt from the 7pt, and empty the 3pt into the 5pt. Now both 5 and 8 contain 4pts.

Topsy-Turvy

The answer is actually trickier for us to hit on nowadays than it would have been originally – it's a nail in a (horse)shoe.

The Wanderer

It is a needle and thread.

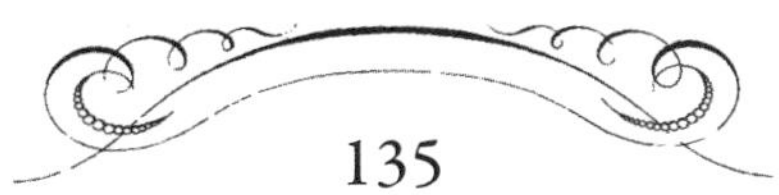

The Hound

The answer is a shoe.

Regiomontanus' Angle

If you draw a circle passing exactly through the top and bottom points of the painting, so that it just touches the eye-level line at one tangential point, that spot where the circle meets the eye-level line is the point of maximum angle width. The distance of this spot from the wall is equal to the square root of the sum of the squares of the height of the top and bottom of the painting.

The Problem of Points

Pacioli's answer, to split the pot according to the number of rounds won up to then, is problematic. What if the game is interrupted after just one or two rounds? It wasn't until Pascal and Fermat started discussing the issue in the 17th century that a good solution was found. The answer is that the division of the pot must depend on the different probable outcomes of the game at that point, rather than on any detail of its history. By working out all the possible remaining outcomes, and tallying which fall to which player, it becomes possible to fairly divide the pot. If one player is 95% certain to win, that player should get 95% of the spoils. A lot of modern probability theory derives from Pascal's and Fermat's work on this puzzle.

 ODESTY

The riddle refers to a walnut.

 URER'S SQUARE

Amazingly, there are 13 different ways to divide the square into four groups of four numbers that sum to 34. These are:

1. Rows,
2. Columns,
3. Diagonals (the numbers orthogonally adjacent to opposing corner squares are the other two groups in this set),
4. Dividing the square into quarters,
5. Taking the top or bottom half of each such quarter with the same section of the quarter below it,
6. Taking the left or right half of each quarter with the same section of the quarter next to it,
7. Taking the top half of each quarter with the bottom half of the quarter diametrically opposed to it,
8. Taking the left half of each quarter with the right half of the quarter diametrically opposed to it,
9. Taking the same cell from each of the four quarters,
10. Taking the same cell from the top two quarters with its diametrically opposed cell in the bottom two quarters,
11. Taking the same cell from the leftmost two quarters with its diametrically opposed cell in the rightmost two quarters,
12. Taking cells clockwise or anti-clockwise from the quarters in turn

as you progress clockwise around them (but to make it trickier, the groups starting top left and bottom right in the top left quarter rotate anticlockwise as you progress, but the other two rotate clockwise), and

13. Taking the central four cells (and the groups of four numbers remaining horizontally, vertically and diagonally).

AN ODD GIFT

The traditional answer is that it is your word.

CLOCK STRIKING PROBLEM

A clock marking the hours will strike 90 times from the first stroke of midday to the last stroke of midnight (or vice versa)

The Dinner Party

If you had a third numeric detail about the men, women and children, you could turn this into a problem of simultaneous equations. As it is, you can reduce one of the terms, and use trial and error on the remaining terms to find the answer. There are 5 men, 3 women and 33 children.

Tricking the Landlord

The simplest approach to this is *Regula Falsi* – start with the landlord first, and then work round to see who is left. Once you know the relative positions of start and end point, it's easy to rotate that round so that the landlord is left. Counting clockwise, with the landlord in position 22, the first person you count should be number 6.

Round and Round

The solution is the sun.

Bachet's Scales

The key to this problem is to think of the possible states that a scale can be in – tipped left, balanced and tipped right. This gives you three possible states. To account for these states, you need to spread your weights in powers of 3. So weights of 1, 3, 9 and 27 are all you need to balance any weight of up to 40, their combined total. For some loads, you'll need to add weights to both sides of the scale, but that is perfectly reasonable. In general, a set of ternary weights like this will allow you to measure up to 150% of the heaviest single weight.

Rupert's Cube

Oddly enough, if you cut your hole across a slanted diagonal of your original cube, you can actually fit a larger cube through it. The maximum size turns out to be ¾ (root 2) – or 1.06 – times the original.

The Newton-Pepys Problem

Pepys' intuitive suspicion was that the largest roll was the easiest. It's not the case, though. You are more likely to make the six-die roll. Newton pointed our that you could imagine the 12-die roll as two sets of the 6-die roll, and the 18-die roll as three sets. To make the 6-die set, you only have to achieve success once. The other sets effectively require you to make the roll more than once. The relative probabilities aren't that simple – you can roll more than 3 sixes in the 18-die roll, at which point you can't quite keep the principle holding true. The 6-die roll has a 0.66 chance, the 12-die roll a 0.62 chance, and the 18-die roll a 0.60 chance.

Sunday

They are going to a funeral. The four men are the pall-bearers; the fifth man is the deceased, in a coffin.

The Tourist

The traditional answer is a watch.

The Bridges of Konigsberg

Euler reasoned that in any network of linked points (usually now known as a graph), each point (node) must either be connected by an even number of lines or an odd number of lines. If you are to be able to walk each line and return to where you started (a 'closed Euler walk'), then you must be able to leave every node you enter – in other words, every node must be even. If you accept starting in one node and ending in a different one, an open Euler walk, there must be exactly two nodes which are odd. If you look at the bridges as a graph, you'll see that there are four nodes (north bank, south bank, big island and small island), and all four have an odd number of lines. No Euler walk is possible.

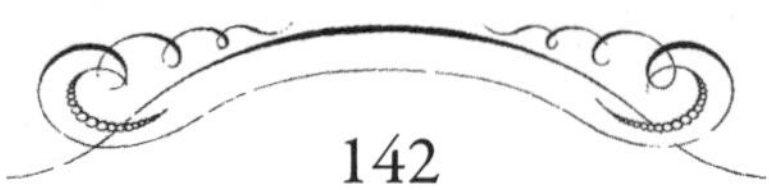

Walking the Walk

In general, the way to find an open Euler walk if you know one is there is to start at a point, move to another by an unused line, and keep going until you run out of room to progress. Then look back over your progress. Somewhere, there will be a node that has an exit you haven't already used. Go back to that and start a new walk, using only lines you have not already used, then splice the new walk into the previous walk. Repeat until the whole graph is covered, and you will have a single composite walk. There are obviously lots of different ways of making a Euler walk in a figure this complex, but one would be as follows: A-D-I-K-J-A-B-C-B-H-C-D-F-I-H-K-F-E-H-G-J-E-A-G.

The Tethered Goat

The goat will be able to move within an oval area bounded by the fence on one side and the radius of its own rope on the other. If the rope is the same radius as the field, the goat will get to the centre of the field, but then be pulled away from the top and bottom. To compensate, and give it enough slack to get to half the area of the field, the rope needs to be longer. (As a point of interest, it needs to be 1.16 the length of the radius of the field).

Buffon's Needle

The chance of any given needle toss crossing a seam depends largely on the angle (x) that the needle makes to the horizontal. The closer the needle to perpendicular, the longer it will seem relative to the perpendicular gap between the lines. This effective length is the sine of the angle of the needle, so solving the specific question of each angle's chance requires solving sin(x). Without getting into the maths too much, sine waves are fundamentally derived from circular motion through time, and Buffon's problem requires the use of pi in order to solve the sine function. In simpler terms, because the angle of the needle varies, the point of the needle effectively becomes a point on a circle (imagine a coin landing between the seams), and this brings pi into the mix, from where it can then be worked out once you know the probability.

The Thunderer

The riddle refers to a shotgun.

OTES